*TMM*PUBLISHING

P.O. Box 5861
Deltona FL 32724
www.TMMPublishing.com

ISBN: 979-8-9914060-5-5

Journey Across The Threshold to Christ

BEYOND
THE
DOORS

DARICK T FISHER

Dedication

To my beloved mother, Brenda D. Fisher,

A devoted wife for over fifty years, a loving mother to four children, and a true servant of God.

Your unwavering faith, love for the Lord, and compassion for people continue to inspire me every day.

This book is a tribute to your life of service, grace, and endless love.

You opened doors of faith and kindness wherever you went, and through this book, I hope to continue your legacy.

I miss you, and I am forever grateful for the lessons you taught me.

With all my love, this is for you.

Acknowledgments

To my bride of 22 years, Venus L. Fisher, thank you for being an amazing wife, my best friend, a wonderful mother, a prayer warrior, and my unwavering support. Your love and encouragement have been my strength, and your faith has been my anchor. You are my greatest cheerleader, and I am endlessly grateful for your presence in my life.

To my four incredible children, Shaniqua, Donye'a, Darick, and Nathanael—you are truly my gifts from God. No matter how old you become, know that I will always cover you in prayer. Thank you for loving me and allowing me to be a part of your lives. Each of you has shaped me in ways that words cannot fully capture. You are the vessels through which the Lord continually molds me, pushing me to be the best father I can possibly be.

You all are my greatest blessings, and I am forever grateful for the love, laughter, and lessons we share. I strive every day to be the example of a loving father that you deserve, and I am honored to walk this journey with you.

With all my heart, thank you.

Endorsement

Darick has a unique way of addressing a host of life challenges. His approach to many of life's problems provides a readable straightforward way to understand how we should deal with many of these life issues. Knowing him for several years and witnessing his life and ministry up close and personally. Has afforded me a rare perspective to view many of his life opportunities clearly articulated through in his practical approach throughout pages of this book.

Jerry A. Gould, DMin

Executive Pastor

All Generations Church

Table of Contents

Preface

"My Journey to the Threshold: From Darkness to Light"

My journey began in the heart of the Bronx, within the walls of Bronx Lebanon Hospital. Born to Donald and Brenda Fisher, I emerged into a world fraught with conflict, mirroring the turmoil of the South Bronx where my childhood unfolded. Despite my roots in a two-parent household with three siblings, Christianity was absent from our home.

I yearned for affection at three or four, but my mother dismissed my sensitivity. By five, rebellion ignited within me, defiance becoming my armor. Yet amidst the chaos, a glimmer of hope emerged as my grandmother introduced me to Christianity, albeit through lengthy church services that left me disenchanted.

By six, craving attention, I lashed out, desperate for recognition. The consequence? Punishment from Big Don, with his faithful friend, the belt. By seven, I delved into premature promiscuity, a cycle persisting through elementary and middle school.

At eight, alcohol entered my world, offering a fleeting escape. By ten years old, my innocence was stolen, a grim introduction to a family member's unspeakable actions.

A pivotal moment arrived during a visit to Portsmouth, Virginia, where illness struck me at the tender age of nine or ten. Helpless and afflicted, my grandmother, great-grandmother, and aunt rallied together in prayer. Miraculously, the sickness dissipated, and in that moment, I accepted Christ as my savior. However, upon returning to the bustling streets of New York City, I succumbed to the allure of worldly pursuits,

1

forsaking my newfound faith. Alcohol and cigarettes became companions in my adolescence, introduced by family members and peers alike.

At eleven, cigarettes became my solace, fueling my growing rebellion. By fifteen, weed seduced me, luring me away from education. Sixteen brought a crossroad: while friends abandoned academia for highs, fear of Big Don kept me anchored. Yet, drugs consumed me, from mescaline to crack cocaine.

As I navigated the tumultuous waters of adolescence, rebellion and defiance became my steadfast companions. From promiscuity to substance abuse, each choice led me further into darkness. Caught in a downward spiral, pregnancies ensued, punctuating my descent. Faced with expulsion from home, I chose the Navy as an escape, only to perpetuate my destructive path.

DUIs and reckless behavior led to incarceration, furthering my descent into despair. Rock bottom arrived, marked by heartache and addiction. In January 1997, I sought solace in Narcotics Anonymous, recognizing my inability to conquer addiction alone. With tears of surrender, I embraced God's unwavering love and mercy, relinquishing the burdens of my past. In 1998, on one rainy day, amidst despair, I cried out to God, surrendering to His embrace. Promising to serve Him, I clung to faith despite my unworthiness. Jesus was no longer just the savior of my life; He was now my Lord and Ruler. This is where the commitment to the journey began. I was no longer straddling the fence between two worlds. I became fully invested in the King and His Kingdom.

In His love, I found redemption. No longer defined by past transgressions, I embraced my identity as a child of the King.

Today, I stand redeemed, restored, and revived. God took my pain and turned it into power for His great purpose: to express His love to all people.

I am Darick T Fisher, a grateful father, loving husband, minister of the Gospel, and public servant. Despite past failures, God orchestrated my redemption, turning darkness into light.

From the bustling streets of the Bronx to a Kingdom citizen on the tranquil shores of Bethlehem, my journey is a testament to the unfathomable depths of God's love and redemption.

Chapter 1:
Crossing the Threshold

Introduction

In the faith journey, seekers often find themselves standing at the threshold, uncertain whether to take a step towards a life in Christ. It is a crucial moment, a turning point where the invitation of the Savior beckons with promises of abundant life. This chapter explores the profound significance of John 10:9 in guiding seekers as they cross the threshold to Christ.

The Threshold of Choice

"I am the door. If anyone enters by me, he will be saved and will go in and out and find pasture." (John 10:9, ESV)

Jesus unfolds the metaphor, portraying Himself as the Shepherd and as the door through which salvation flows. Crossing this threshold is not merely a physical act but a profound decision rooted in the depths of the heart and soul. It unfolds as a spiritual struggle, where the natural inclinations of the flesh engage in a tug of war with the beckoning of our spiritual essence, orchestrated by the Holy Spirit. The act of crossing this threshold is not merely a physical movement but a symbolic representation of a deeper, internal conflict—a dynamic interplay between the tangible and the spiritual, between the worldly and the divine. It signifies a choice that involves surrendering the desires of the flesh to the higher calling of the Holy Spirit, ultimately leading to a transformative journey into the spiritual realm.

A Shepard named Donovan.

In the vibrant heart of New York City, where the rhythm of life resonates through the concrete canyons and the subway's symphony hums beneath the surface, there lived a shepherd named Donovan. Unlike traditional shepherds, Donovan found his flock not in meadows and hills but in the city's diverse neighborhoods and busy streets. His flock comprised people from all walks of life, seeking solace and guidance during the urban chaos.

One evening, as the sun dipped below the skyscrapers and the city's neon lights began to sparkle, Donovan gathered his eclectic group near a subway station in Times Square. He pointed towards the subway car door, its metallic surface gleaming with the reflections of the city lights, an unexpected portal to something extraordinary.

"My brother and sisters," Donovan proclaimed above the urban cacophony, "this is the entrance to a realm of potential and purpose. The opportunities beyond are vast, and the challenges are conquerable. But to enter, you must pass through this door."

The melting pot of people looked at the subway car door, some curious and others uncertain. Donovan walked towards the door, swiped his metro card, and the doors slid open, revealing the illuminated path of the subway tunnel.

"I am the door," (reciting the words of Christ in John 10:9) Donovan declared, his words weaving through the echoes of the subway station, "If anyone enters by me, they will be saved from the mundane and will traverse the tunnels of destiny."

The people approached the subway car door one by one, crossing the threshold into the promised journey. As they entered, a sense of anticipation and purpose enveloped them. The subway car, adorned with the city's graffiti and filled with the rhythmic clatter of the tracks, became a vessel of transformation.

Donovan watched over his flock, as a Shepard does for his sheep, grateful they had trusted him enough to board this metaphorical train into a new chapter of their lives. And so, under the watchful guidance of their shepherd, the diverse group of people navigated the twists and turns of the subway tunnels, finding fulfillment in the journey they had undertaken through the subway car door.

Understanding the Doorway

Jesus' self-proclamation as the door signifies more than just access; it implies a transformative passage. The threshold is not merely an entrance but a gateway to a new reality. By entering through Him, believers experience salvation, a rebirth that marks the beginning of a journey filled with purpose and divine guidance. As the door, Jesus signifies the exclusive and essential pathway to salvation and a life filled with hope and promise. This life is not without difficulties, problems, and conflict. The reality is that, with or without Christ, humanity will go through these challenges anyway. I have concluded that if this is our reality, I will exchange my old life for His.

This exchange between humanity and Christ involves an act of faith, surrender, and humility where individuals acknowledge Jesus as the only means of salvation. By entering through Him, one finds deliverance from self-reliance and gains the freedom to go in and out, symbolizing a dynamic, intimate relationship with Christ. This exchange is an invitation to experience the fullness of life and spiritual nourishment that only Christ, the Door, can provide.

Salvation Beyond the Threshold

The promise of salvation is not confined to a single moment but extends beyond the threshold into a life of abundance. This ongoing sanctification process is a lifelong journey, much like the perpetual motion of a subway car coursing through the intricate web of tunnels beneath the city.

As the diverse assembly, under Donovan's guidance, crossed the subway car door's threshold, they found themselves immersed in a journey that mirrored the complexities of life. The subway's rhythmic clatter became a metaphor for the continuous rhythm of growth and transformation in their spiritual lives.

The subway tunnels, with their twists and turns, echoed the challenges and uncertainties of life Donovan, the shepherd, stood at the center of the subway car, much like Jesus, the Shepherd, who promised to go before His sheep and lead them beside still waters. As the urban explorers ventured "in and out" on this journey, they discovered a dynamic relationship with their shepherd that went beyond the forgiveness of sins.

Donovan's voice resonated through the subway car, offering guidance, encouragement, and wisdom. The metaphorical pasture extended beyond the subway tunnels, revealing itself in the diverse neighborhoods and opportunities of the city. The bustling streets became the vibrant pastures where the city's souls found nourishment and purpose.

The subway journey was not without challenges. There were moments of darkness, symbolic of life's trials, but Donovan's words reassured them. "I am the door," he declared, "and through me, you will find light even in the darkest tunnels."

As the subway car emerged into the brightness of another station, Donovan continued to lead the group through the threshold of each new experience. The city's tapestry unfolded before them, offering a rich and varied landscape for growth. The promise of going in and out and finding pasture took on new meaning as the urban explorers engaged with the city's diverse culture, contributing their unique gifts to the world.

The subway journey represented a physical movement and a spiritual pilgrimage, with Donovan as the guiding shepherd. The assembly experienced the abundance of life promised beyond the threshold through the challenges, uncertainties, and triumphs. The subway car door became a symbol of entry and ongoing transformation, a portal to a dynamic relationship with the Shepherd who provided, guided, and protected on life's journey.

Certainty of Christ: A Journey Across the Threshold (John 14:6)

As Donovan led his diverse assembly through the intricate subway system of New York City, a subtle murmur of doubt began to echo among some of his followers. The city, with its multitude of doors and pathways, each claiming to lead to something significant, sparked uncertainty in the hearts of a few.

"Is Donovan truly the only way?" whispered one, glancing at the array of subway exits, each beckoning with its own promises.

These doubts reached Donovan's ears, and he paused in the middle of the subway car. His eyes, filled with compassion, met those of the questioning souls. He understood the weight of their concerns, for the city indeed boasted numerous doors, each presenting an enticing path.

With a calm demeanor, Donovan addressed the assembly, drawing inspiration from the timeless words found in John 14:6: "I am the way, the truth, and the life. No one comes to the Father except through me."

"My friends," he began, "I understand that the city is filled with doors, each claiming to be the way. But remember, it's not about the door itself but what lies beyond. In the same way, I guide you through the subway tunnels to a richer, purposeful life; Jesus is the way to an eternal and fulfilling relationship with God."

He continued, weaving his words with reassurance and conviction, "Christ's statement isn't a declaration of exclusivity but an invitation to certainty. In this intricate city, where confusion and doubt may arise, Jesus provides a clear path. Just as I guide you through the subway, He guides us to a deeper understanding of life and purpose."

Donovan's words resonated with the assembly as the subway car traversed the labyrinth of tunnels. The doubts that had clouded a few minds began to dissipate, replaced by a sense of assurance that transcended the multitude of doors in the city.

"The certainty of Christ is not a rigid dogma but a liberating truth," Donovan emphasized. "It's a journey across the threshold of doubt into the certainty that God, through Christ, has provided the way to a meaningful and eternal life."

The subway journey became not just a physical movement through the city but a spiritual pilgrimage, a collective understanding that, despite the myriad doors and paths, Christ's way offered certainty in the midst of uncertainty. The diverse assembly, now reinvigorated with faith, continued their subway pilgrimage with a newfound assurance in the certainty of Christ.

Bold Declaration: Embracing the Exclusive Way in John 14:6

"Jesus said to him, 'I am the way, and the truth, and the life. No one comes to the Father except through me.'" (John 14:6, ESV)

Embarking on the Life changing journey of faith, as outlined in John 14:6, hinges on a fundamental belief that demands the full measure of trust. In this sacred declaration, Jesus not only presents Himself as the door and the way but emphasizes the indispensable role of faith in recognizing Him as the sole path to the Father.

Acknowledging the exclusive way in John 14:6 is not merely an intellectual ascent but a comprehensive trust acknowledging Jesus as the exclusive and singular way to the Father. It requires believers to embrace the profound truth that salvation and access to the Father are found solely through Christ. This holistic faith encompasses a conviction that there is no alternative route or substitute, demanding a complete surrender to the exclusive claim of Jesus as the way, the truth, and the life.

Faith begins with an unwavering recognition of Jesus as the door. This acknowledgment is not just an understanding of salvation as a concept but a deep trust that Jesus alone provides the secure refuge needed for eternal safety. Crossing the threshold demands a faith that finds assurance in the door of Christ, relying on Him exclusively for deliverance from the perils of sin and separation from God.

According to John 14:6, faith propels believers along the illuminated path of truth. It is not a one-time act but an ongoing journey marked by a commitment to walk daily in the footsteps of Christ. The way, as revealed through His teachings and life, becomes the trajectory of faith, guiding believers through the complexities of life. This journey necessitates an unwavering trust that every step in faith aligns with the exclusive path to the Father.

Exclusive faith, rooted in John 14:6, becomes the compass navigating life's challenges. It involves trusting that, even amid trials, uncertainties, and tribulations, the exclusive way of Christ remains a steadfast guide. Faith assures believers that the exclusive truth of Jesus is not just a claim but a tangible source of strength, leading them through every obstacle toward the ultimate destination—the Father's presence.

In the profound journey of faith outlined in John 14:6, believers are invited to embrace an exclusive trust, acknowledging Jesus as the only way to the Father. This faith is not just a belief system but a transformative journey, starting with the door of salvation and continuing along the illuminated path of truth. May this exclusive faith inspire believers to walk confidently in the assurance that, through Christ alone, they find their way to the Father.

Crossing the threshold requires exclusive faith – a deep trust in the Shepherd who stands at the door. Faith is the key that unlocks the life-changing power of salvation. Believers are called to trust in Jesus for their eternal destiny and the abundant life He promises in the present.

Challenges Beyond the Door

Amidst the diverse neighborhoods and bustling streets of New York City, Donovan's assembly continued their subway journey, facing challenges that tested the depth of their faith. The promise of abundant life, spoken of in John 10:9 and further emphasized in John 10:10, became a beacon of hope amidst the urban trials. Once a symbol of entry into a vibrant existence, the subway car door became a metaphor for the thresholds of life's difficulties. There were moments when the journey through the city's landscape felt like navigating through dark tunnels. Financial hardships, relational complexities, and the relentless pace of the urban grind threatened to overshadow the promise of abundance.

Donovan, however, stood firm as their shepherd. He drew inspiration from John 10:9, reminding his followers that their challenges were not insurmountable. "Through this door," he declared, "we find sustenance even in the most trying times. The Shepherd's promise extends beyond the comfort of the subway car; it permeates the very fabric of our lives."

Drawing from John 10:10, he continued, "The thief comes only to steal and kill and destroy; I have come that they may have life and have it to the full." Donovan stressed that the challenges encountered were the handiwork of the thief, seeking to steal their peace, kill their joy, and destroy their hope. Yet, the promise of abundant life offered by the Shepherd stood as a resilient force against the adversity they faced.

As doubts resurfaced among some followers, Donovan again turned to the words of John 14:6 to address the challenges of uncertainty. The city, with its myriad doors and conflicting ideologies, presented a maze of spiritual options. "There may be many doors in this city, each claiming to be the way," Donovan spoke, his voice resolute. "But the certainty of Christ is our anchor in the face of uncertainty. Jesus is not just a door; He is the way, the truth, and the life. During the confusion, His clarity guides us through the complexities of this concrete jungle landscape."

The challenges beyond the subway doors, reflective of life's trials, became an opportunity for the assembly to deepen their understanding of the certainty found in Christ. Each obstacle encountered was met with the assurance that, through Christ, they had the strength to overcome. As the subway journey continued, Donovan's followers, now seasoned travelers through the city's challenges, embraced the dual promises of John 10:9, John 10:10, and John 14:6. The subway car door became a symbol of entry, perseverance, and triumph. Through the twists and turns of life, Donovan's followers found abundance and certainty, guided by the Shepherd who led them beyond the challenges and uncertainties of the urban landscape.

Conclusion

Crossing the threshold does not exempt believers from challenges. Instead, it assures them of the constant companionship of the Shepherd. As they navigate the complexities of existence, the door through which they enter salvation transforms into a sanctuary in times of trouble and a wellspring of strength in moments of weakness. The Shepherd, who guided them into this transformational relationship, remains steadfast, offering peace and empowerment. The challenges encountered beyond the door serve as opportunities for growth, resilience, and a deepening reliance on the Shepherd's unwavering care. In facing adversity, believers discover that the threshold they crossed becomes a symbol of assurance—a reminder that, with the Shepherd Jesus Christ by their side, they are equipped to overcome obstacles, find refuge, and experience the abundant life promised by the Good Shepherd in John 10:10.

Chapter 2:
Trap Door Part One

5 Stages of Enticement

Temptation: The Proposition Stage

James 1:14 (NIV) - "Tempted when by his OWN evil desires."

The gentle ripples on the lake mirrored the subtle stirrings within Emily's soul. Standing on the shore, her gaze fixed on the tranquil waters, she couldn't escape the truth that our flesh harbors a desire for sin and things that aren't of the LORD. It was the first proposition stage, akin to a fisherman noticing the wriggling worm on his hook.

In the quiet of her thoughts, the lure of the bait became apparent. The metaphorical worm dangled before Emily's consciousness, tempting and enticing. It wasn't an external force but a realization that her own desires, like the wriggling worm on the fisherman's hook, yearned for attention. The awareness of this internal bait marked the inception of temptation, a gentle invitation that beckoned her toward the depths of her own desires.

Galatians 5:16-17 (NIV) - "So I say, walk by the Spirit, and you will not gratify the desires of the flesh. For the flesh desires what is contrary to the Spirit, and the Spirit what is contrary to the flesh. They conflict with each other, so you are not to do whatever you want."

The sun dipped below the horizon, casting a warm glow over the quiet lake. As Emily strolled along the water's edge, the timeless truth echoed in her mind – in its very nature, the flesh harbors a desire for sin and things contrary to the Lord. It was a spiritual tension between the flesh's desires and the Spirit's guidance, much like a fisherman casting his line into the waters.

In the stillness of her thoughts, Emily recognized the subtle dance between the desires of her flesh and the Spirit's call. The metaphorical worm on the fisherman's hook represented the allure of sin, a tangible manifestation of the conflict within. The bait dangled before her consciousness, a choice between walking by the Spirit or gratifying the desires of the flesh. The realization of this internal struggle marked the inception of temptation, a gentle invitation to navigate the delicate balance between the conflicting forces within her.

Emily stood at the edge of a serene lake, surrounded by the gentle rustling of leaves and the distant calls of birds. The tranquil scene belied the internal struggle echoing the conflict described in Galatians 5:16-17.

"So I say, walk by the Spirit," whispered a soft voice carried by the breeze that rippled across the water. It was a call to navigate the calm depths of the lake, aligning herself with a divine guide beyond the surface tranquility.

"And you will not gratify the desires of the flesh," the voice continued, promising a serene haven away from the ripples of temptation that danced upon the lake. Emily recognized the lure of temptation, not in the city lights, but in the subtle movements beneath the water's surface – a realm where the desires of the flesh swam, enticing her attention.

The lake's allure was strong, its depths holding secrets and the promise of fleeting pleasure. The flesh's desires, like elusive fish, flickered just beneath the surface, vying for her attention. Yet, beneath the calm waters, Emily sensed a deeper conflict.

The flesh desired what was contrary to the Spirit, like hidden currents beneath the lake's surface. It was a gentle undercurrent that threatened to carry her away into the enticing world of earthly desires – a world where the fisherman's bait danced, promising fulfillment.

"And the Spirit, what is contrary to the flesh," echoed the voice, a counterpoint to the siren call of the lake's depths. Amidst the natural beauty, Emily felt a pull towards something greater – a spiritual yearning that sought fulfillment beyond the transient pleasures of the lake.

"They conflict with each other," the voice reminded her, cautioning against being swept away by the conflicting currents. Emily stood at the water's edge, torn between the promises of the lake's depths and the call of the Spirit. The lake stretched before her, each ripple leading to a different destination.

"So that you are not to do whatever you want," concluded the soft voice, a sobering reminder that unchecked desires could lead to a path devoid of spiritual fulfillment. The tranquil lake became a metaphorical fishing ground, and Emily, amidst the rippling waters, faced a choice – to walk by the Spirit or to succumb to the alluring desires that swam beneath the surface.

In the midst of nature's symphony, Emily's internal struggle mirrored the timeless conflict described in Galatians 5:16-17, a narrative of choices and consequences that unfolded against the backdrop of the serene lake.

Enticed: The Deliberation Stage - The Gentle Tug James 1:14 (NIV) - "He is dragged away and enticed.

The moonlight bathed the lake in a silver glow, casting a mesmerizing reflection on the water's surface. Emily stood at the water's edge, the gentle tug of temptation beginning to weave its intricate dance around her conscience.

"He is dragged away and enticed," whispered the night breeze, carrying the weight of a decision waiting to be made. The metaphorical worm on the fisherman's hook had been noticed, and the subtle allure of the forbidden taste lingered in the air.

As Emily contemplated the shimmering waters, the tug on her heart mirrored the gentle pull on a fisherman's line when a fish showed interest in the bait. Thoughts, like ripples on the lake, radiated from the center of her being. The pros and cons of indulging in the desire began to unfold in her mind.

The taste of justification crept in as she talked herself through the internal debate. "The LORD will forgive me," she reassured herself, feeling the subtle satisfaction of rationalization. The internal dialogue became a dance, a delicate negotiation between the pull of desire and the voice of reason.

The lake, once a symbol of serenity, now mirrored the conflict within Emily's soul. She stood at the crossroads, aware she could still run or swim away, escaping the impending choice. The tension in the air held the promise of consequences and the allure of the forbidden, much like a fish contemplating the worm on the hook.

The choice lay before her, suspended in the stillness of the night. The shimmering waters, now a canvas for the reflection of her internal struggle, awaited the decision that would send ripples through the fabric of her conscience. In this deliberation stage, the gentle tug of temptation played out its dance, urging Emily to decide – to swim away from the allure or to embrace the enticing taste of the forbidden worm.

The moonlit lake mirrored the dance of temptation within Emily's soul. The verse from 1 Corinthians 10:13 echoed softly in her thoughts, becoming a compass in the quietude of the night. 1 Corinthians 10:13 "13 No temptation has overtaken you except such as is common to man; but God is faithful, who will not allow you to be tempted beyond what you are able, but with the temptation will also make the way of escape, that you may be able to bear it." (NKJV)

"No temptation has overtaken you except such as is common to man," whispered the divine reassurance, wrapping Emily in the understanding that her struggles were shared among humanity. The realization brought a certain comfort as if the weight of her internal conflict was not an anomaly but a universal experience.

"But God is faithful," continued the gentle voice, a reminder that divine steadfastness stood as an anchor amidst the swirling currents of her temptations. The lake, reflecting the vastness of the night sky, seemed to echo this faithfulness, weaving the constancy of the Creator into the fabric of her contemplation.

"He will not allow you to be tempted beyond what you can," the reassurance deepened, creating a sense of boundaries within her struggles. It was as if the moonlit waters whispered that the depths of her temptation were known and accounted for by a benevolent force.

"But the temptation will also make the way of escape," the voice added, becoming a beacon of hope in the shadows of her thoughts. Once a mere setting, the lake transformed into a landscape of choices and possibilities. Each ripple on the water hinted at a way out, a divine escape route intricately woven into the fabric of her internal struggle.

"That you may be able to bear it," concluded the verse, a promise that the burdens of temptation were not meant to crush her. Rather, the lake's gentle lapping against the shore reflected the understanding that she was equipped to withstand the trials, guided by the divine assurance in the scripture.

As Emily stood by the water's edge, the gentle tug of temptation persisted, but now she carried with her the profound truth of 1 Corinthians 10:13. The lake, once a battleground, became a sanctuary where the dance of the night reflected not only the struggles within but also the unwavering promise that, with divine guidance, every temptation carried within it a way of escape. The gentle tug, now softened by the assurance of

God's faithfulness, beckoned Emily to consider the allure of the bait and the boundless grace that surrounded her.

Lust Conceived: The Buy-in Stage

James 1:15 (NIV) - "Then after desire is conceived."

The moon hung low in the velvety night sky, casting a subtle glow on the lake's rippling surface. Emily, at the water's edge, felt the weight of the night deepen as she wrestled with the words, "Then after desire is conceived."

The gentle tug of temptation had morphed into a decisive undertow, pulling her into the buy-in stage. The verses from James 1:15 echoed in her thoughts as she stood at the precipice of choice. The once-distant allure of the metaphorical worm on the hook had transformed into a tangible need, a craving that echoed in the quiet recesses of her being.

Emily's mind became a battleground, a theater of acceptance where the narrative of yielding replaced the script of resistance. Once a symbol of tranquility, the lake became the reflective canvas for the shifting tides within her. Each ripple seemed to echo the internal dialogue, the pros and cons playing out in the subtle movements of the water.

The verses collided with the moment as Emily found herself taking deliberate steps, closing the door to her inner sanctum. The quiet shores bore witness to her acceptance, a silent agreement with the desires that had, until now, only whispered in the corridors of her thoughts.

Reaching out to the metaphorical bottle, the lake mirrored her actions, the moonlight casting a somber glow on the scene. Emily had traversed from the deliberation stage to the acceptance stage, where thoughts materialized into actions. The metaphorical worm was no longer just an enticing idea but a tangible need, and with each passing moment, her resolve solidified.

The buy-in stage unfolded like the turning of a key in a lock, the choice to indulge in the desires of the flesh, closing the door on alternatives. The night seemed to hold its breath, awaiting the outcome of Emily's internal struggle.

In this pivotal moment, the verses lingered in the air, a poignant reminder that a way of escape persisted even at the buy-in stage. The lake, a silent witness to the drama of choices, awaited the ripples that would follow - the consequences of decisions made in the night's quietude.

Sin Birthed: The Commencement Stage

The lake, once a serene witness to the quiet battles of the night, now mirrored the turmoil within Emily's soul. The verses from James 1:15, "It gives birth to sin," echoed in the stillness, a haunting reminder of the cascade that followed the buy-in stage.

Standing on the water's edge, Emily felt the heaviness of the choice made in the buy-in stage. The ripple effect of her decision extended across the tranquil lake, distorting its once-mirrored reflections. As she uncorked the metaphorical bottle, the night seemed to shudder, and the moonlight dimmed as if nature itself lamented the birth of sin.

The commencement stage unfolded like the unraveling of a tragic drama. The lake, once a canvas of serene beauty, now bore witness to the shadows cast by Emily's choices. With each sip, the metaphorical worm became a bitter reality, its taste staining the purity of the water.

Like ripples on the lake, Emily's actions created a dissonance in the once-harmonious night. The moon, obscured by a passing cloud, seemed to withdraw its glow as if unable to illuminate the darkness that descended upon the acceptance-turned-commencement stage.

The verses lingered in the air, a spectral reminder that every birthed sin carried the weight of consequences. The night, once a sanctuary, transformed into a stage where the drama of choices played out. The lake, a reluctant audience, reflected the distortions caused by Emily's plunge into the depths of her desires.

In the sin-birthed stage, the silence was pierced by the echoes of regret, the realization that the acceptance stage had given birth to actions irreversible. The once-clear waters now swirled with the murkiness of remorse, each sip drawing her further into the depths of a choice that stained the lake's surface and the sanctity of her soul.

As the night embraced the sin-birthed stage, Emily, caught in the currents of her own decisions, found herself adrift in the consequences of the choices that had unfolded on the quiet shores of the moonlit lake.

Death: The Verdict Stage

The lake, once a tranquil haven, now bore witness to the aftermath of Emily's choices. The echoes of James 1:15, "Sin when it is full-grown, gives birth to death," reverberated across the water, a somber reminder of the ultimate consequence of her actions.

As Emily stood on the shore, the weight of her decisions pressed upon her like the oppressive night. The moon, now obscured behind thick clouds, seemed to mourn the loss of innocence that had unfolded on its shores. The once-clear waters now reflected the darkness that enveloped her soul.

In the verdict stage, Emily felt the weight of condemnation descends upon her like a heavy cloak that suffocated her spirit. The verses from Romans 6:23, "For the wages of sin is death," whispered in the wind, their chilling truth cutting through the night air.

The lake, once a mirror of clarity, now reflected the distorted image of Emily's guilt-stricken face. Each ripple in the water seemed to mock her, a reminder of the irreversible consequences of her actions. The metaphorical bottle, now emptied of its contents, lay discarded on the shore, a silent testimony to the folly of indulgence.

As Emily grappled with the verdict stage, she felt the weight of her decisions bearing down upon her. The verses from Hebrews 9:27, "And as it is appointed for men to die once, but after this the judgment," resonated within her, stirring a sense of dread at the thought of facing the consequences of her actions.

The lake, once a sanctuary of peace, now seemed to reflect the specter of death that loomed over Emily's soul. The silence of the night was broken only by the echoes of remorse, a haunting lament for the life lost to the grip of sin.

In the verdict stage, Emily stood on the precipice of reckoning, her heart heavy with the burden of guilt. The verses from Romans 14:12, "So then each of us shall give an account of himself to God," hung in the air, a sobering reminder that every action would be weighed in the balance of divine justice.

As the night wore on, Emily felt the chill of judgment seep into her bones, a harbinger of the death that awaited her soul. She stood alone in the quiet of the moonlit lake, a testament to the devastating consequences of allowing sin to take root and flourish.

Redemption: The Turning Point

As Emily stood on the desolate shore, weighed down by the burden of her choices, a faint glimmer of hope pierced the darkness of her despair. The verses from 1 John 1:9 whispered in the wind, "If we confess our sins, He is faithful and just to forgive us our sins and to cleanse us from all unrighteousness."

During judgment's grip, Emily felt a flicker of realization ignite within her soul. Like a beacon in the night, the promise of forgiveness illuminated the path back to redemption. The verses from Psalm 103:12 echoed in her mind, "As far as the east is from the west, so far has He removed our transgressions from us."

Tears mingled with the moonlit waters as Emily bowed her head in contrition, her heart heavy with remorse. The verses from Isaiah 1:18 seemed to resonate within her, "Though your sins are like scarlet, they shall be as white as snow; though they are red like crimson, they shall be as wool."

With trembling hands, Emily reached out to the heavens, her voice trembling as she uttered a prayer of repentance. The verses from Acts 3:19 filled her with renewed hope, "Repent therefore and be converted that your sins may be blotted out, so that times of refreshing may come from the presence of the Lord."

In that moment of surrender, Emily felt the weight of judgment lift from her shoulders, replaced by the gentle embrace of divine grace. The verses from Ephesians 2:8-9 echoed in her heart, "For by grace you have been saved through faith, and that not of yourselves; it is the gift of God, not of works, lest anyone should boast."

As Emily stood on the shore, her spirit renewed by the promise of forgiveness, she felt a sense of peace wash over her like the gentle tide. The verses from Romans 8:1 reassured her, "There is now no condemnation to those who are in Christ Jesus, who do not walk according to the flesh, but according to the Spirit."

In the stillness of the night, Emily's soul found solace in the embrace of divine love. With each breath, she felt the burden of her past mistakes lift, replaced by the freedom found in the forgiveness of her Heavenly Father. As she walked away from the lake, her heart overflowing with gratitude, Emily knew that though she had stumbled into the depths of sin, she had been lifted by the boundless mercy of God.

Let us look at the story of Licking the Knife

By Island Times staff

Eskimos trap wolves for their fur. They make warm and beautiful coats. Here's how they kill a wolf, Eskimo Style. Up in the Arctic Circle, there is a tribe of Eskimos who have learned to set a very simple yet effective trap for wolves. First, they sharpen a knife razor sharp. Then, they dip it in the blood of a seal they have killed. (You see, seals are fairly easy to trap, but wolves are very dangerous). After dipping the knife in blood, they set it outside in the cold so the blood freezes on the knife. After it freezes (a matter of minutes), they dip it again into the seal blood, take it out, and let it freeze. Layer after layer, they make a blood popsicle. The knife's blade is hidden inside when they are done, just like a popsicle stick. Now, they take the knife out into the wilderness, where they think a wolf might be. There, they bury the knife handle in the snow, leaving the blood popsicle standing up there, and then leave.

Now, after a while, a wolf will come along guided by his sense of smell and find the "bloodsicle." He will be licking it, enjoying every taste. Over and over, he licks the knife, and soon, his tongue is so cold he cannot feel it any longer. It's numb. But his taste for blood is growing, and he is not getting as much as he wants – you see, popsicles are slow eating. Finally, his licking exposes the razor-sharp edge of the knife. It cuts into his tongue repeatedly, but he does not even notice, for his tongue can no longer feel anything. The wolf's own blood now flows from his cut tongue. The wolf is thrilled. With the blood now more plentiful and warm, he continues to lick more and more.

Soon, he notices something is wrong, and he is getting weaker, not stronger. Since he knows blood as food, he increases his efforts to feed on the ever-increasing flow of blood. His last thoughts are of how good the now warm blood tastes. Within minutes, he licks his last and collapses next to the now fully exposed knife. Here, the Eskimo knows he will find the wolf's body the next morning. The hungry wolf died of exsanguination.

The story of the wolf and the trap is a chilling analogy to the concept outlined in James 1:13-15. In Emily's story, titled "Trap Door," the fishing analogy mirrors the stages of temptation outlined in James 1:13-15. Similarly, the wolf's encounter with the bloodsicle trap reflects the stages of temptation leading to sin and death.

In the wolf's case, the trap is set with a seemingly enticing bait – the bloodsicle. This resembles Emily's story, where the worm on the fisherman's hook represents the lure. The wolf, driven by its natural instinct and desire for blood, falls victim to the trap, much like how Emily succumbs to the allure of temptation.

As the wolf continues to lick the bloodsicle, its senses become dulled, and it becomes oblivious to the danger posed by the hidden razor-sharp knife. Similarly, in Emily's story, as she progresses through the stages of temptation, her judgment becomes clouded, and she becomes increasingly unaware of the consequences of her actions.

Ultimately, just as the wolf's insatiable desire for blood leads to its demise, Emily's indulgence in temptation leads to spiritual death. The trapdoor analogy in Emily's story serves as a cautionary tale, illustrating the destructive nature of succumbing to temptation and the importance of recognizing the escape routes provided by God in moments of trial. Both stories serve as sobering reminders of the need to remain vigilant against sin's allure and seek refuge in God's grace and forgiveness.

A Choice in the Wilderness

As Emily walked away from the lake, her heart weighed down by the gravity of her past actions, she found herself at a crossroads, much like Aron Ralston in the gripping tale of "127 Hours." Both faced pivotal moments where a choice had to be made, a choice that would shape their destinies.

Just as Aron Ralston had been trapped in a remote canyon, Emily had been ensnared in the wilderness of temptation, each facing a life-or-death decision. The echoes of Matthew 5:22-30 reverberated in her mind, reminding her of the gravity of her choices and their consequences.

In Matthew 5:27-28, Jesus spoke of the seriousness of lustful thoughts, equating them with the act of adultery itself. Just as Aron Ralston faced the reality of his predicament in the canyon, Emily confronted the harsh truth of her temptation. The metaphorical knife of sin lay hidden beneath the surface, waiting to ensnare her in its deadly grip.

As Aron Ralston had ultimately chosen to amputate his own arm to escape the canyon, Emily faced a similar choice – to sever the ties that bound her to temptation and sin. The verses from Matthew 5:29-30 spoke of the radical action required to overcome temptation, likening it to gouging out one's eye or cutting off one's hand.

Emily grappled with the weight of her decisions in the wilderness of temptation. Just as Aron Ralston had summoned the courage to make the agonizing choice to free himself from the canyon, Emily resolved to confront her past mistakes and seek forgiveness.

With the verses from Matthew 5 as her guide, Emily made the courageous decision to confront the temptations that threatened to trap her soul. She reached out to trusted friends and mentors, seeking accountability and guidance on the path to healing and redemption.

As she embarked on her transformation journey, Emily knew the road ahead would be fraught with challenges. But she also knew that she was not alone, that God's grace and mercy would sustain her every step of the way.

Just as Aron Ralston emerged from the canyon transformed by his experience, Emily emerged from the wilderness of temptation with a renewed sense of purpose and a deepened faith in the power of redemption.

Rescue in the Wilderness

As Emily walked away from the lake, her heart lighter and the burden of guilt lifted, she found herself confronted with yet another choice, reminiscent of the harrowing decision faced by Aron Ralston in the true story of "127 Hours."

Just as Emily had faced the temptation stages outlined in James 1:13-15, Aron Ralston had found himself trapped in a remote canyon, forced to make a life-or-death decision. Emily's journey through the wilderness of temptation led her to a moment of reckoning, where she had to choose between continuing on the path of destruction or seeking redemption and rescue.

In a moment of clarity, Emily recalled the lessons learned from the scriptures and the promise of forgiveness and redemption. She remembered the verses from Psalm 34:17-18, "The righteous cry out, and the Lord hears them; he delivers them from all their troubles. The Lord is close to the brokenhearted and saves those crushed in spirit." With renewed resolve, Emily decided to seek help and salvation.

Just as Aron Ralston had ultimately chosen to amputate his own arm to free himself from the canyon, Emily made the courageous choice to confront her past mistakes and seek forgiveness. She reached out to trusted friends and mentors, sharing her struggles and seeking guidance on the path to healing and restoration.

The parallel between Emily's story and Aron Ralston's ordeal served as a poignant reminder of the power of choice and the resilience of the human spirit. Both faced seemingly insurmountable obstacles, yet they found the strength to make the difficult decisions necessary for survival and redemption.

As Emily embarked on her journey of healing and renewal, she knew that the road ahead would not be easy. But she also knew that she was not alone, that God's grace and mercy would guide her every step of the way. Just as Aron Ralston had emerged from the canyon transformed by his experience, Emily emerged from the wilderness of temptation with a newfound sense of purpose and a deepened faith in the power of redemption.

Chapter 3
Trap Door Part 2

Proverbs 7:1-27 ESV

My son, keep my words and treasure my commandments with you; keep my commandments and live; keep my teaching as the apple of your eye; bind them on your fingers; write them on the tablet of your heart. Say to wisdom, "You are my sister," and call insight your intimate friend, to keep you from the forbidden woman, from the adulteress with her smooth words. For at the window of my house, I have looked out through my lattice, and I have seen among the simple, I have perceived among the youths, a young man lacking sense, passing along the street near her corner, taking the road to her house in the twilight, in the evening, at the time of night and darkness. And behold, the woman meets him, dressed as a prostitute, wily of heart. She is loud and wayward; her feet do not stay at home; now in the street, now in the market, and at every corner, she lies in wait. She seizes him and kisses him, and with a bold face, she says to him, "I had to offer sacrifices, and today I have paid my vows; so now I have come out to meet you, to seek you eagerly, and I have found you. I have spread my couch with coverings, colored linens from Egyptian linen; I have perfumed my bed with myrrh, aloes, and cinnamon. Come, let us take our fill of love till morning; let us delight ourselves with love. My husband is not at home; he has gone on a long journey; he took a bag of money with him; at full moon, he will come home. "With much seductive speech she persuades him; with her smooth talk, she compels him. All at once he follows her, as an ox goes to the slaughter, or as a stag is caught fast till an arrow pierces its liver; as a bird rushes into a snare, he does not know that it will cost him his life. And now, O sons, listen to me, and be attentive to the words in my mouth. Let not your heart turn aside to her ways; do not stray into her paths, for many a victim has she laid low, and all her slain are a mighty throng. Her house is the way to Sheol, going down to the chambers of death.

Let us now take a sneak peek into Theodore's life.

The Allure of Temptation

The bustling streets of Hollywood, California, were a stage for dreams and desires, where ambitions collided with the seductive allure of success. Among the hopefuls seeking their big break in the entertainment industry was Theodore, a young aspiring actor with stars in his eyes and a hunger for fame. As Theodore navigated the glitzy world of Hollywood, he found himself drawn into a web of temptation, mirroring the pitfalls described in Proverbs 7. The streets teemed with allure, promising fame, fortune, and fulfillment yet concealing the subtle traps that lay in wait for the unsuspecting.

Treasure God's Commandments: In the heart of Hollywood's glamour, Theodore felt the weight of Proverbs 7:1, urging him to treasure God's commandments. Amidst the dazzle of fame and fortune, he remembered the moral compass that guided his upbringing, now challenged by the allure of worldly success. In a town where success was often measured by wealth and fame, he understood that true treasure lay in valuing the teachings of his faith above all else.

Keep God's Words as the Apple of Your Eye: The glittering lights of Hollywood beckoned Theodore to keep God's words as the apple of his eye, as Proverbs 7:2-3 cautioned. Amidst the flashing cameras and whispered promises, he tried to cling to the truths instilled in him, guarding against the deceptive allure of the entertainment industry. In a place where image was everything, he knew he must keep God's words at the forefront of his mind, guiding him in pursuing what truly mattered.

Bind God's Commandments on Your Fingers: In the heart of Tinseltown's temptation, Theodore needed to bind God's commandments on his fingers, as Proverbs 7:3 suggested. With each script offered and each audition attended, he sought to remain grounded in the principles of righteousness, refusing to compromise his values for success. Like a ribbon tied around his fingers, God's commandments were to be a constant reminder of his commitment to living a life of righteousness.

Write God's Wisdom on the Tablet of Your Heart: As Theodore navigated the cutthroat world of Hollywood, he sought to write God's wisdom on the tablet of his heart, as Proverbs 7:3 urged. Theodore felt the truth of these words sinking deeper into his soul with each passing moment. It wasn't enough to simply know God's wisdom; he must internalize it, allowing it to shape his desires and intentions. Only then could he resist the allure of sin that beckoned from the bright lights of Hollywood. Among the whispers of compromise and the allure of instant gratification, he clung to the timeless truths that anchored his soul, seeking to walk in integrity and honor.

Call Understanding and Insight Your Closest Kin: In the midst of Hollywood's allure, Theodore embraced understanding and insight as his closest kin, as Proverbs 7:4-5 encouraged. Amidst the glamour and glitz, he leaned on discernment and wisdom to navigate the treacherous waters of temptation, seeking to honor God in all he did. Theodore found comfort in the companionship of understanding and insight. With their guidance, he knew he could discern right from wrong, navigating the treacherous waters of Hollywood with clarity and purpose.

Subtitle: Subtle Temptation (Proverbs 7:6-9)

Things took a turn for Theodore as he found himself entangled in the web of subtle temptation, mirroring the scenario described in Proverbs 7:6-9. In the heart of Hollywood's hustle and bustle, he encountered the alluring whispers of compromise and opportunity, beckoning him with promises of fame and success.

The Simple and Lacking Sense: Solomon describes the young man as simple and lacking sense. This simplicity leaves him vulnerable to the subtle allure of temptation. Proverbs 14:15 reinforces this idea: "The simple believe anything, but the prudent give thought to their steps." It emphasizes the importance of discernment in avoiding the snares set by deceptive temptations.

Like the naive young man described in Proverbs 7:7, Theodore found himself vulnerable to the subtle allure of temptation. Despite his aspirations and dreams, he lacked the discernment to see through the facade of worldly success, falling prey to the cunning schemes that lay in wait.

The Cunning Approach of Temptation: Proverbs 6:24 provides insight into the cunning approach of temptation: "keeping you from your neighbor's wife, from the smooth talk of a wayward woman." This verse highlights the deceptive nature of temptation, often presented in an appealing and alluring manner, drawing individuals away from God's intended path. Theodore was taken aback by the cunning approach of temptation, as described in Proverbs 7:8. The offers of easy fame and instant gratification seemed irresistible, cloaked in the guise of opportunity and advancement. Despite the warnings echoing in his mind, he found himself drawn closer to the enticing allure of compromise.

The Lure of Sinful Pleasures: As Theodore ventured further into the world of Hollywood, he found himself ensnared by the lure of sinful pleasures, echoing the scenario depicted in Proverbs 7:9. The parties, the glitz, and the glamour seemed to offer a taste of the high life, closing his eyes to the consequences of his actions and leading him further down the path of temptation.

Despite the warnings of Proverbs 7 ringing in his ears, Theodore felt himself being swept away by the current of subtle temptation, unsure of how to extricate himself from its grasp.

As he grappled with the allure of compromise and the whispers of opportunity, he knew that the choices he made in the coming days would shape the trajectory of his life in ways he could scarcely imagine. Theodore felt the tug of desire as he considered the sinful pleasures that awaited him if he were to accept the invitation. He knew the risks, yet the allure of excitement and indulgence whispered sweetly in his ear. Ecclesiastes 7:26 flashed through his mind, a sobering reminder of the bitter consequences that awaited those who fell prey to the snares of temptation.

With a heavy heart, Theodore recalled the words of Proverbs 4:23—the foundational scripture on guarding the heart. As he wrestled with the allure of temptation and the subtle whispers of compromise, he realized the critical importance of protecting his heart from the snares of sin.

Theodore understood that the heart was the wellspring of life, the source from which all his thoughts, desires, and actions flowed. He knew that safeguarding his heart was to protect the essence of who he was—to preserve his integrity, values, and relationship with God amidst the enticing allure of worldly success.

Proverbs 4:23 echoed in Theodore's mind like a beacon of light in the midst of darkness, reminding him of the proactive role he must take in guarding his heart against the subtle deceptions of temptation. He understood that it was not enough to resist temptation when it presented itself merely; he must also cultivate a lifestyle of vigilance and discernment, actively seeking to fortify his heart with the truth of God's Word and the power of His Spirit.

As Theodore reflected on the importance of guarding his heart, he resolved to take deliberate steps to protect himself from the snares of sin. He committed to saturating his mind with Scripture, filling his heart with praise and worship, and surrounding himself with fellow believers who could provide accountability and support in his journey.

Theodore set his sights on the path of righteousness with a renewed sense of purpose and determination. He thought he was ready for the task ahead, knowing that true fulfillment could only be found in walking in obedience to God's commands. Despite the challenges and temptations that lay ahead, he trusted in the promise of Proverbs 4:23—that as he guarded his heart with diligence, God would grant him the strength and wisdom to navigate the treacherous waters of temptation and emerge victorious on the other side.

Seductive Allure Proverbs 7:10-12

As Theodore continued his journey through the convoluted streets of Hollywood, he found himself trapped by the seductive allure described in Proverbs 7:10-12. Like a moth drawn to a flame, he was lured deeper into the web of temptation, captivated by the promise of fame and success that seemed to shimmer just out of reach.

The streets pulsated with energy, neon lights casting an ethereal glow over the bustling crowds. Amidst the hopefuls and dreamers, Theodore felt a sense of exhilaration mingled with apprehension, knowing that every step he took brought him closer to the edge of the precipice.

As he wandered through the labyrinth of studios and clubs, Theodore found himself surrounded by a whirlwind of sights and sounds—the laughter of strangers, the flash of cameras, the tantalizing aroma of decadent cuisine. Each sensation seemed to beckon him further into the heart of temptation, blurring the lines between reality and illusion.

Proverbs 7:10-12 echoed in Theodore's mind like a haunting refrain, a warning of the danger that lurked just beyond the glitz and glamour of Hollywood. Yet, despite the cautionary tale woven into the fabric of Scripture, he could not resist the siren call of worldly success.

Theodore was acutely aware of the subtle allure surrounding him—the promises of wealth, adoration, and acclaim that seemed to hang like ripe fruit waiting to be plucked. Despite the warning signs flashing in his mind, he felt a growing sense of excitement and anticipation, eager to taste the forbidden pleasures within his grasp.

As he surrendered to the seductive allure of temptation, Theodore felt a thrill course through his veins—a rush of adrenaline that swept away his doubts and fears. At that moment, he was intoxicated by the promise of what could be, blinded to the consequences that lurked just beneath the surface.

With each step he took, Theodore ventured further into the heart of temptation, unaware of the traps waiting for the unsuspecting. Little did he know that his chosen path would lead him down a path fraught with peril, where the promise of success would ultimately give way to despair and disillusionment.

The Temptress's Approach. Theodore's heart quickened as he recalled the words of Proverbs 7:10-12, which described the approach of the temptress with vivid detail. He pictured her lurking in the shadows, her sultry gaze and smooth words weaving a web of enticement around him. The subtlety of her seduction was both alluring and dangerous, drawing him ever closer to the edge of temptation.

Theodore's heart raced as he stood on the precipice of surrender, the allure of temptation pulling him ever closer to the edge. Despite the warning bells ringing in his mind, he was teetering on the brink of folly, unable to resist the seductive whispers that beckoned him further into the abyss.

Proverbs 5:3-4 NIV echoed in Theodore's thoughts like a solemn warning from a distant voice, urging him to heed the wisdom of the ages:

"For the lips of the adulterous woman drip honey,
and her speech is smoother than oil;
but in the end, she is bitter as gall,
sharp as a double-edged sword."

Theodore felt a chill run down his spine as he contemplated these words—a sobering reminder of his treacherous path. The allure of temptation seemed to grow stronger with each passing moment, its grip tightening around his heart like a vice.

Despite the warning signs flashing in his mind, Theodore was drawn inexorably towards the enticing promises that lay before him. The prospect of fame and success seemed to shimmer like a mirage in the desert, tantalizingly close yet impossibly distant.

In that moment of vulnerability, Theodore found himself grappling with a choice that would shape the course of his destiny. Would he yield to the seductive allure of temptation, surrendering his principles and integrity in exchange for fleeting pleasures? Or would he muster the strength to resist, clinging to the timeless truths that had guided him thus far?

As Theodore stood at the crossroads of decision, he felt a flicker of hope ignite within his soul—a glimmer of light amidst the encroaching darkness. With a determined resolve, he squared his shoulders. He steeled himself against the temptation that threatened to engulf him, knowing that the path of righteousness was fraught with peril but ultimately led to everlasting life.

With each step he took toward the temptress's lair, Theodore felt a sense of urgency rising within him. The weight of Proverbs 4:14-15 pressed upon his heart like a heavy burden, urging him to resist the allure of temptation and to turn away from the path of destruction:

> *"Do not set foot on the path of the wicked,*
> *or walk in the way of evildoers.*
> *Avoid it, do not travel on it,*
> *turn from it and go on your way."*

As Theodore contemplated these words, he felt a surge of conviction coursing through his veins—a renewed determination to resist the temptations that threatened to ensnare him. Despite the tantalizing promises that lay before him, he knew the path of righteousness was the only way to true fulfillment and peace.

With each passing moment, the urgency of resistance grew stronger within Theodore's heart. He could feel the pull of temptation tugging at his soul, enticing him with promises of pleasure and satisfaction. Yet, he refused to be swayed by the fleeting temptations of the flesh, knowing that true satisfaction could only be found in walking in alignment with God's will.

As he stood on the threshold of temptation, Theodore consciously chose to heed the wisdom of Proverbs 4:14-15. With a resolute spirit, he turned away from the path of wickedness and set his feet firmly on the road of righteousness, determined to pursue a life of integrity and honor.

Though the journey ahead would be overwrought with challenges and obstacles, Theodore knew he was not alone. With God as his guide and protector, he faced the temptations of Hollywood with unwavering faith and courage, trusting in the promise that those who resist the temptations of sin will find strength and refuge in the arms of the Lord.

Enticement of Flattery

As Theodore probed deeper into the heart of Hollywood's allure, he found himself ensnared by the enticement of flattery, echoing the scenarios depicted in Proverbs 7:15-18. The glitz and glamour of Tinseltown whispered promises of fame and fortune, tempting him with visions of success and adoration.

In the midst of the neon-lit streets and bustling crowds, Theodore encountered the allure of flattery in every corner. Hollywood's seductive voice beckoned him with promises of stardom, painting a picture of a life filled with luxury and acclaim.

Proverbs 7:15-18 echoed in Theodore's mind like a haunting melody, weaving a web of temptation and deceit:

"So I came out to meet you;
I looked for you and have found you!
I have adorned my set
with the finest decorations from around the world.
I have scented the air
with the most exquisite fragrances.
Come, let's indulge in success till dawn;
let's revel in the spotlight together!"

Theodore began to listen to the flattering words of Hollywood; he felt a stirring within his soul—a longing for recognition and validation that threatened to cloud his judgment and lead him astray. The promises of fame and adoration seemed almost irresistible, drawing him ever closer to the edge of temptation.

Despite the warning bells ringing in his mind, Theodore found himself mesmerized by the flattery of Hollywood, unable to resist the allure of its promises. The lavish offers of wealth and prestige seemed to hold him captive, closing his eyes to the consequences of his actions and leading him further down the path of deception.

In that moment of vulnerability, Theodore felt a battle raging within him—a conflict between the flesh's desires and his heart's convictions. Though he knew that Hollywood's promises were laced with deceit and manipulation, he found himself struggling to resist the tantalizing allure that beckoned to him with outstretched arms.

As Theodore stood at the crossroads of decision, he knew that his choices in the coming moments would shape his destiny. Would he succumb to the enticement of flattery, surrendering his integrity and honor in exchange for fleeting fame? Or would he find the strength to resist, clinging to the timeless truths that had guided him thus far?

With a prayer on his lips and determination in his heart, Theodore resolved to resist the enticement of flattery and to stand firm in his commitment to righteousness. Though the journey ahead would be fraught with challenges and temptations, he knew he was not alone. With God as his strength and refuge, he faced the allure of Hollywood with unwavering faith and courage, trusting in the promise that those who resist the temptations of sin will find deliverance and victory in the end.

While Theodore wrestled with the allure of Hollywood's promises, he found solace in recalling the struggles of the Apostle Paul, as recounted in Romans 7. The echoes of Paul's battle with sin resonated deeply within Theodore's own heart, reminding him that he was not alone in his struggle against temptation.

In the pages of Romans 7, Theodore found a mirror reflecting his inner turmoil—a battle between the flesh's desires and the spirit's convictions. Like Paul, he grappled with the tension between what he knew to be right and the allure of worldly pleasures that beckoned him with their enticing promises.

When Theodore dwelled on Paul's words, he found himself nodding in recognition at the Apostle's lament:

"For I do not understand what I am doing. I do not do what I want, but I do the very thing I hate... For I have the desire to do what is right but not the ability to carry it out. For I do not do the good I want, but the evil I do not want is what I keep on doing." (Romans 7:15,18-19)

In those words, Theodore found a reflection of his own struggles—a recognition of the inner conflict that raged within him, tearing at the fabric of his resolve and leaving him feeling helpless and alone. Yet, amidst the despair and frustration, he also found a glimmer of hope—a reminder that even the greatest of saints had wrestled with the same struggles and emerged victorious through the grace of God.

With a renewed sense of determination, Theodore resolved to follow in the footsteps of Paul—to press on in the face of temptation, trusting in the power of God's Spirit to strengthen him and guide him on the path of righteousness. With Paul as his companion in struggle and God as his ever-present help, Theodore faced the allure of Hollywood with courage and faith, knowing that victory awaited those who persevered until the end.

The Temptress's Persuasion

When Theodore continued to struggle with the allure of Hollywood's promises and the echoes of Paul's struggles, he found himself confronted by the persuasive words of the temptress. Like a skilled seductress, she spun a web of persuasion, weaving a tapestry of deceit and temptation that threatened to trap him completely.

With each word she spoke, Theodore felt the tendrils of her persuasion winding around his heart, clouding his judgment and stirring up desires he knew he should resist. Her promises of fame and success seemed to shimmer like mirages in the desert, tantalizingly close yet impossibly out of reach.

The temptress's persuasion echoed in Theodore's mind like a hypnotic mantra, luring him deeper into the labyrinth of temptation:

"Come, Theodore, and taste the sweet nectar of success. Let me adorn you with the trappings of fame and fortune, and together, we will revel in the spotlight, basking in the masses' adoration. Do not resist; I offer you a life beyond your wildest dreams—a life of luxury, indulgence, and pleasure."

While Theodore listened to her honeyed words, he felt a tug-of-war raging within his soul—a battle between the yearnings of his flesh and the convictions of his spirit. Though he knew the temptress's promises were built on a foundation of lies and deceit, he struggled to resist the allure of her persuasion, drawn to the promise of instant gratification and worldly acclaim.

In that moment of vulnerability, Theodore realized the gravity of the choice before him. Would he succumb to the temptress's persuasion, surrendering his integrity and honor in exchange for fleeting pleasures? Or would he find the strength to resist, clinging to the timeless truths that had guided him thus far?

With a prayer on his lips and the echoes of Paul's struggles ringing in his ears, Theodore resolved to stand firm against the temptress's persuasion. Though the road ahead would be fraught with challenges and obstacles, he knew he was not alone. With God as his strength and refuge, he knew he could face the allure of Hollywood if he stayed submitted to Him. He continued to journey with unwavering faith and courage, trusting in the promise that those who resist the temptations of sin will find deliverance and victory in the end.

The Allure of False Promises

Theodore stood at the crossroads of decision, grappling with the allure of false promises surrounding him. The words of Proverbs 26:28 reverberated in his mind like a warning bell:

"A lying tongue hates those it hurts, and a flattering mouth works ruin."

He knew the temptress's persuasion was built on a foundation of deceit and manipulation, designed to lead him astray and ultimately bring about his downfall. Yet, despite the warning signs flashing in his mind, he felt the pull of temptation growing stronger with each passing moment.

In the midst of his inner turmoil, Theodore recalled the danger of yielding to temptation, as outlined in Proverbs 2:16-19:

"Wisdom will save you also from the adulterous woman, from the wayward woman with her seductive words, who has left the partner of her youth and ignored the covenant she made before God. Surely, her house leads down to death and her path to the spirits of the dead. None who go to her return or attain the paths of life."

Theodore felt a chill run down his spine as he contemplated these words—a sobering reminder of his perilous path. The temptress's false promises led only to destruction and despair, offering temporary pleasures that would ultimately lead to ruin.

With a renewed sense of resolve, Theodore consciously resisted the allure of false promises and clung to the wisdom of God's Word. Though the temptations of Hollywood loomed large before him, he knew that true fulfillment could only be found in walking in alignment with God's will.

The Temptation of Forbidden Pleasures Proverbs 7:19-20

The struggle continued for Theodore as he found himself trapped by the temptation of forbidden pleasures, a modern-day reflection of the scenario depicted in Proverbs 7:19-20. The allure of indulgence and excess beckoned to him, promising fleeting satisfaction while concealing the dire consequences that awaited.

With his heart racing, Theodore grappled with the seductive whispers of temptation, and he felt the weight of Proverbs 7:19-20 bearing down upon him like a heavy burden:

"The man's wife is a trap, and her talk is a snare. The temptress lures you with her flattery, appealing to your emotions and leading you to ruin."

The temptations of Hollywood seemed to surround Theodore at every turn, each offering a tantalizing glimpse of pleasure and gratification. Yet, he knew deep down that yielding to these forbidden pleasures would only lead him further down the path of destruction, separating him from the truth and light he had once embraced.

During his inner turmoil, Theodore wrestled with the conflicting desires of his heart. On one hand, the allure of forbidden pleasures promised momentary satisfaction and pleasure. On the other, the wisdom of God's Word urged him to resist, warning of the pitfalls that awaited those who yielded to temptation.

With a heavy heart and a troubled spirit, Theodore solemnly vowed to stand firm against the temptations surrounding him. He knew that he could not afford to compromise his integrity and values for the sake of temporary pleasures. Hebrews 11:25-26 began to resonate deeply within his heart:

"He chose to be mistreated along with the people of God rather than to enjoy the fleeting pleasures of sin. He regarded disgrace for the sake of Christ as a greater value than the treasures of Egypt because he was looking ahead to his reward."

Theodore found solace and inspiration in those verses as they illuminated a path of unwavering commitment and faithfulness. Like the heroes of faith described in Hebrews, he realized that true fulfillment could not be found in the fleeting pleasures of the world but in the enduring promises of God.

As Theodore reflected on these words, he felt a renewed sense of purpose and determination coursing through his veins. With a resolute spirit and unwavering faith, Theodore resolved to follow in the footsteps of those who had gone before him, choosing to endure hardship and persecution rather than yield to the temptations of sin.

Severe Consequences (Proverbs 7:21-23)

Just as Theodore began to feel a sense of victory over the temptations that had plagued him, he found himself ensnared in the trap of severe consequences, echoing the sobering reality depicted in Proverbs 7:21-23:

"With persuasive words, she led him astray; she seduced him with her smooth talk. All at once, he followed her like an ox going to the slaughter, like a deer stepping into a noose till an arrow pierces his liver, like a bird darting into a snare, little knowing it will cost him his life."

Theodore's heart sank as he realized the gravity of his situation. Despite his best efforts to resist temptation, he had fallen prey to the deceitful allure of Hollywood, succumbing to the smooth talk and flattery that had ensnared so many before him.

Theodore's sense of freedom was shattered in an instant, replaced by a profound sense of regret and despair. He felt like an ox led to slaughter, a deer caught in a trap, a bird ensnared by a hunter's snare—powerless to escape the consequences of his actions.

As he grappled with the weight of his choices, Theodore knew he could not undo the past. The consequences of his actions loomed large before him, casting a shadow over his once bright future.

He continues to ponder Proverbs 7:22: "All at once he followed her like an ox going to the slaughter, like a deer stepping into a noose."

The simplicity of his yielding to the temptations of Hollywood struck him with painful clarity. As a naive animal led to its demise, Theodore had blindly followed the enticing promises of fame and pleasure, oblivious to the traps that awaited him.

In hindsight, Theodore saw the folly of his choices. The allure of temporary pleasures had closed his eyes to the long-term consequences, leading him down a path of destruction and despair. He realized that the shackles of sin were not forged instantly but through a series of seemingly small and insignificant decisions that ultimately culminated in his downfall.

With a heavy heart, Theodore acknowledged his own vulnerability and fallibility. He understood that the simple act of yielding to temptation could have far-reaching consequences, leading him further away from the path of righteousness and truth.

He truly felt like prey being hunted down and killed and couldn't shake the feeling described in Proverbs 7:23: "Till an arrow pierces his liver, like a bird darting into a snare, little knowing it will cost him his life." He felt like prey being hunted down and killed, ensnared by the consequences of his foolish actions.

With each passing moment, the words of Proverbs 5:22 echo in his mind: "The evil deeds of the wicked ensnare them; the cords of their sins hold them fast." Theodore realized that he had become entangled in the web of his own transgressions, held fast by the cords of sin that threatened to suffocate him.

In the depths of his despair, Theodore understood the gravity of his situation. He had allowed himself to be lured away from the path of righteousness, falling victim to the deceptive schemes of the enemy. Now, like a bird caught in a snare, he found himself trapped, unable to escape the consequences of his actions.

As he wrestled with guilt and remorse, Theodore knew he couldn't undo the past. The judicious outcome of his foolish actions loomed large before him, casting a shadow over his once hopeful future.

Yet, despite his despair, Theodore clung to a glimmer of hope. He knew that God's mercy was limitless and that there was still a chance for redemption and renewal even in his darkest hour.

Separation and the Call to Wisdom (Proverbs 7:24-27)

As Theodore tussled with the overwhelming power of sin and the consequences of his actions, he found himself searching desperately for a way out of the trap that had ensnared him. Amid his turmoil, the words of Proverbs 7:24-27 resonated deeply within his soul:

"Now then, my sons, listen to me; pay attention to what I say. Do not let your heart turn to her ways or stray into her paths. She has brought many victims; her slain is a mighty throng. Her house is a highway to the grave, leading down to the chambers of death."

These words echoed in Theodore's mind like a beacon of hope amidst the darkness. They served as a stern reminder of the perilous consequences of yielding to temptation and straying from the path of righteousness. Theodore understood the urgency of these words. He knew that he could not afford to continue down the path of sin and destruction, for it led only to death and despair. Yet, despite his best efforts to break free, he found himself trapped by the power of temptation, unable to find a way out on his own.

With a renewed sense of determination, Theodore consciously decided to separate himself from the seductive allure of Hollywood's sinful pleasures. He understood that true freedom could only be found in heeding the call to wisdom, turning away from the glittering façade of fame and fortune that masked the dangers lurking beneath. As he took steps to distance himself from the temptations that had once held him captive, Theodore felt the weight of his burdens begin to lift. Theodore felt the chains of sin loosening their grip on his soul.

Theodore heard the call to wisdom ringing clear and true in the depths of his despair. He realized that true freedom could only be found in heeding the voice of wisdom and turning away from the path of sin and destruction.

Each passing moment in Hollywood brought Theodore closer to a newfound sense of purpose and resolve. As he clung to the promise of protection that awaited those who heeded the call to wisdom, he found solace in the words of Proverbs 7:26-27:

"For she has cast down many wounded, and all who she slew were strong men. Her house is the way to hell, descending to the chambers of death."

These verses served as a stark reminder of the dangers that lurked in the shadows of the entertainment industry, where the pursuit of fleeting pleasures and empty promises had shattered countless lives. Yet, Theodore found strength in knowing he was not alone in his struggle. With God as his protector, he faced the trials and temptations of Hollywood with unwavering faith and courage.

As Theodore continued his journey of separation from the snares of sin, he found himself guided by the pathway to freedom illuminated by the timeless wisdom of Proverbs 3:5-6:

"Trust in the LORD with all your heart and lean not on your own understanding; In all your ways acknowledge Him, and He shall direct your paths."

These words became his guiding light, leading him away from the pitfalls of temptation and toward a brighter future filled with hope and possibility. With each step he took in faith, Theodore felt the burdens of his past begin to lift, replaced by a renewed sense of purpose and direction.

Theodore held onto the hope of restoration in the depths of his heart, knowing that God's grace was sufficient to redeem even the most broken of lives. Though the road ahead would be challenging, he faced it with confidence, trusting in the promise of God's unfailing love and mercy to carry him through to the end.

As Theodore continued his journey through the glittering streets of Hollywood, he did so with a newfound sense of peace and determination. With God as his guide and protector, he knew that he was destined for greater things and that no obstacle or temptation could stand in the way of the hope and restoration that awaited him.

Seeking The Lord Isaiah 55:6

Theodore found solace and direction in the words of Isaiah 55:6, which echoed the urgency of seeking the Lord while He may be found. These words reinforced the principle of responding promptly to divine wisdom, reminding him of the importance of seeking God's guidance and presence in every aspect of his life.

As he reflected on these words, Theodore realized the necessity of repentance for true restoration. He understood that seeking the Lord was not merely a matter of convenience but a crucial step towards healing and renewal. With a repentant heart and a humble spirit, he sought forgiveness for his past mistakes and shortcomings, knowing that God's grace was sufficient to cover even the most egregious sins.

In the quiet moments of reflection, Theodore found himself drawn closer to the heart of God. He felt a sense of peace and assurance wash over him, knowing that he was not alone in his journey towards restoration. With each step he took in faith, he felt the burdens of his past being lifted, replaced by a renewed sense of hope and purpose.

As Theodore continued to seek the Lord with all his heart, he found himself transformed from the inside out. His eyes were opened to the beauty of God's love and the depth of His mercy, and he experienced a joy and peace that surpassed all understanding.

With each passing day, Theodore's relationship with God grew stronger, and he found himself walking in the freedom and restoration that only He could provide. He knew that his journey was far from over, but with God by his side, he faced the future with confidence and courage, knowing that the best was yet to come. Yet, despite his despair, Theodore clung to a glimmer of hope. He knew that God's mercy was limitless and that there was still a chance for redemption and renewal even in his darkest hour.

The Power of Redemption. Theodore stood at the crossroads of temptation and remembered the promise of redemption that awaited those who turned back to the Lord. With a prayer on his lips and resolve in his heart, he turned away from the seductive allure of sin and chose instead to walk in the light of God's truth. Though the road ahead would be difficult, he trusted in the promise of God's forgiveness and grace, knowing that he could overcome even the most dire of circumstances with faith and perseverance.

Chapter 4

Revolving Doors Part One

A revolving door typically means a door consisting of several horizontal panels rotating around a vertical axis within a cylindrical enclosure. It's often used at building entrances to control the flow of people entering and exiting while minimizing drafts and noise. Metaphorically, it can represent a situation where there is a constant turnover cycle, such as in employment or relationships. In relationships, a revolving door could describe a pattern where individuals repeatedly enter and exit relationships with different partners. It suggests a cycle of starting new relationships, encountering challenges or conflicts, and ending the relationship only to repeat the process with someone new.

Revolving Door Relationship

In a revolving door relationship, there's a sense of cyclical behavior where individuals repeatedly enter and exit each other's lives, often encountering similar challenges or issues each time they reconnect.

Let us take a peek into the Character of Gollum.

Originally named Sméagol, Gollum is one of the most complex characters in J.R.R. Tolkien's "The Lord of the Rings." Here's an overview of his background and characteristics:

Background:

Early Life as Sméagol:

Sméagol was once a Hobbit-like creature from a river-dwelling community, living a relatively normal life. While fishing with his cousin Déagol on his birthday, Sméagol discovered the One Ring when Déagol found it in the river. Overcome by its power, Sméagol murdered Déagol to obtain the Ring. Transformation into Gollum: The Ring's corrupting influence transformed Sméagol into the creature known as Gollum. His family and community drove him out, and he took refuge in the Misty Mountains.

He lived in the dark caves for centuries, calling the Ring his "Precious" and gradually losing his sanity and humanity.

Characteristics:

Dual Personality:

Gollum has a split personality: one side is the malevolent "Gollum" who is obsessed with the Ring and willing to do anything to possess it, while the other side is the pitiable "Sméagol" who still retains some remnants of his former self.

This duality is often portrayed in internal dialogues where the two sides argue and struggle for control.

Relationship with the Ring:

Gollum's life is entirely dominated by his obsession with the Ring, which he calls his "Precious." The Ring's power prolongs his life and causes immense suffering and madness.

His obsession makes him pitiable and dangerous; he is willing to betray, deceive, and even kill to reclaim it.

Encounter with Bilbo:

Gollum first appears in "The Hobbit" during Bilbo Baggins' journey. Bilbo finds the Ring and inadvertently engages in a game of riddles with Gollum. Bilbo eventually escapes with the Ring, setting the stage for the events in "The Lord of the Rings."

Journey with Frodo and Sam:

In "The Lord of the Rings," Gollum becomes important when he follows Frodo and Sam, trying to reclaim the Ring.

Frodo shows him kindness and tries to bring out the Sméagol side, while Sam remains suspicious and distrustful of him.

Gollum guides Frodo and Sam to Mordor but eventually succumbs to his darker nature.

Final Fate:

Ultimately, Gollum's obsession with the Ring leads to his downfall. At Mount Doom, he attacks Frodo and bites off his finger to reclaim the Ring.

In his elation, he falls into the fires of Mount Doom, destroying the Ring and himself, ultimately bringing about the Ring's destruction and the defeat of Sauron.

Gollum's character is a powerful representation of the corrupting influence of power and the internal struggle between good and evil. His tragic story adds depth and complexity to the overarching narrative of "The Lord of the Rings."

Gollum is often alone, consumed by his obsession with the One Ring. He frequently rationalizes his actions and blames others, particularly Frodo and Sam, for his misfortunes. His dual personality reflects his internal struggle and the excuses he makes for his behavior. His isolation and self-pity, along with his tendency to make excuses. The story of Gollum in "The Lord of the Rings" shares several thematic parallels with the man at the Pool of Bethesda from the Bible (John 5:1-15). These parallels primarily revolve around themes of isolation, excuses, longing for change, and the impact of transformative encounters.

John 5:1-15 NIV

Some time later, Jesus went up to Jerusalem for one of the Jewish festivals. Now there is in Jerusalem near the Sheep Gate a pool, which in Aramaic is called Bethesda and which is surrounded by five covered colonnades. Here, a great number of disabled people used to lie—the blind, the lame, the paralyzed. One who was there had been an invalid for thirty-eight years. When Jesus saw him lying there and learned that he had been in this condition for a long time, he asked him, "Do you want to get well?" "Sir," the invalid replied, "I have no one to help me into the pool when the water is stirred. While I am trying to get in, someone else goes down ahead of me."

Then Jesus said to him, "Get up! Pick up your mat and walk." At once, the man was cured; he picked up his mat and walked. The day this took place was a Sabbath, and so the Jewish leaders said to the man who had been healed, "It is the Sabbath; the law forbids you to carry your mat." But he replied, "The man who made me well said to me, 'Pick up your mat and walk.'" So they asked him, "Who is this fellow who told you to pick it up and walk?" The man who was healed man had no idea who it was, for Jesus had slipped away into the crowd that was there. Later, Jesus found him at the temple and said to him, "See, you are well again. Stop sinning, or something worse may happen to you." The man went away and told the Jewish leaders that it was Jesus who had made him well. '

Let us examine a few of these parallels!

Physical Isolation: Gollum lived in the dark caves of the Misty Mountains for centuries, separated from any community. His obsession with the One Ring led him to a life of solitude.

Emotional Isolation: Even when he was with Frodo and Sam, Gollum was fundamentally alone. His dual personality created an internal isolation where he was at constant war with himself.

Man at the Pool of Bethesda:

Physical Isolation: The man had been at the Pool of Bethesda for thirty-eight years, unable to move himself into the healing waters. He was surrounded by others in need but lacked any personal assistance.

61

Emotional Isolation: His prolonged illness and inability to find help left him feeling despondent and disconnected, much like Gollum's detachment from others due to his long isolation.

Making Excuses

Gollum:

Rationalizations: Gollum often made excuses to justify his actions. He blamed others for his misfortunes and rationalized his treachery as necessary to regain the Ring. He would say things like, "They stole it from us," and, "We want it. We need it. Must have the precious."

Internal Conflict: His inner dialogue is filled with justifications for his behavior, reflecting his inability to take responsibility for his actions and change his ways.

Man at the Pool of Bethesda:

Excuses for Inaction: When Jesus asked if he wanted to be healed, the man responded by saying, "I have no one to help me into the pool when the water is stirred. While I am trying to get in, someone else goes down ahead of me" (John 5:7). Instead of directly expressing his desire for healing, he highlighted his helplessness and the obstacles he faced.

Longing for Change

Gollum:

Desire for the Ring: Gollum's obsession with the Ring represents his desire to reclaim a part of his past. However, this desire keeps him trapped in a cycle of dependence and destruction, preventing any real change or redemption.

Moments of Clarity: Occasionally, the Sméagol side of his personality surfaces, showing a longing for connection and change. These moments are fleeting but indicate a deep-seated desire for something better.

Man at the Pool of Bethesda:

Desire for Healing: Despite his excuses, the man's presence at the pool for many years shows a persistent hope for change. He longed for healing and a different life, but his circumstances and mindset kept him trapped.

Transformative Encounter

Gollum:

Encounter with Frodo: Frodo's compassion towards Gollum brings out moments of Sméagol, suggesting the potential for transformation. However, Gollum ultimately succumbs to his darker nature, unable to break free from the Ring's hold.

Failure to Change: Unlike the man at the Pool of Bethesda, Gollum's encounters fail to bring lasting change, highlighting the tragedy of his character.

Man at the Pool of Bethesda:

Encounter with Jesus: The transformative moment for the man comes when Jesus tells him, "Get up! Pick up your mat and walk" (John 5:8). This command empowers the man to overcome his paralysis and excuses, leading to immediate healing and a new life.

Success in Transformation: The man's story concludes with a successful transformation, contrasting with Gollum's tragic end.

Conclusion:

While Gollum and the man at the Pool of Bethesda differ in their ultimate outcomes, both stories explore the deep impacts of isolation (lack of friendship) and the struggle to overcome one's circumstances. Gollum's narrative highlights the tragic consequences of failing to overcome internal and external demons, while the man at Bethesda's story emphasizes the redemptive power of transformative encounters and the importance of seizing the opportunity for change. Both characters illustrate the profound human experiences of loneliness, making excuses, and the hope (or tragedy) inherent in pivotal moments of transformation.

In "The Lord of the Rings: The Return of the King," Gollum (Sméagol) makes statements that reflect his isolation and tendency to make excuses. One of the most telling lines is during a moment of inner conflict where Gollum talks to himself, highlighting his dual nature and the excuses he makes to justify his actions.

Here's a passage from the book that showcases this aspect of his character:

"We be nice to them if they are nice to us," said Gollum. "We are nice to them, very nice if they are nice to us." "It's still trying to cheat us; it's doing its best to get us to let our guard down," said the other voice. "And what has it got in its pockets?" "Precious, precious, precious! We want it. We need it. Must have the precious. They stole it from us. Sneaky little hobbits. Wicked, tricksy, false!"

Here is another statement from "The Lord of the Rings: The Two Towers" film,

Nobody likes you; the master is my friend. Leave now and never come back".

Relationships are vital in humanity's lives. The quality of the relationship will shape a person's destiny. Speaking of destiny, let us explore the journey of Destiny and how the Revolving doors have shaped her life.

Revolving Doors

In the heart of Clearwater, Idaho, nestled between the whispering pines and the gentle curves of the Clearwater River, lived a woman named Destiny. Her life was a series of revolving doors, constantly spinning between isolation and fleeting moments of connection, much like the legends of old that echoed through her small town.

Early Life and Isolation

Destiny's early years were filled with warmth and family, but tragedy struck when she lost her parents in a car accident. This loss left her feeling abandoned and utterly alone, like Sméagol from the ancient tales. Sméagol, who, after finding the One Ring, transformed into the wretched Gollum, driven by obsession and isolation. As Gollum retreated to the dark caves, Destiny withdrew into her small cabin on the outskirts of Clearwater, seeking solace in solitude. Proverbs 18:1 says, "An unfriendly person pursues selfish ends and against all sound judgment starts quarrels," highlighting how isolation can skew one's perspective and actions.

Her life mirrored the man at the Pool of Bethesda, described in John 5:1-15. Like the man who lay by the pool for thirty-eight years, waiting for someone to help him into the healing waters, Destiny waited for something—or someone—to pull her out of her despair. "I have no one to help me into the pool," the man had said (John 5:7), and Destiny, too, felt the sting of friendlessness and helplessness. This echoed the isolation felt by Elijah when he said, "I have been very zealous for the LORD God Almighty... I am the only one left, and now they are trying to kill me too" (1 Kings 19:10).

The Pool of Bethesda in Clearwater

Clearwater had its own legend of a healing spring, much like the Pool of Bethesda. The townspeople believed the waters could cure ailments, but Destiny never visited. She dismissed the idea as foolishness, an excuse to avoid confronting her fears and loneliness. She often thought, "Even if I went, no one would help me," justifying her isolation with every passing day.

Her days she has revolved around this cycle of self-imposed exile and excuses. Each day began and ended with the same thoughts, spinning endlessly like revolving doors that led nowhere. Destiny's isolation deepened, and her heart grew heavier, burdened by the weight of missed opportunities and unrealized hopes.

A Chance Encounter

One crisp autumn day, as Destiny foraged for mushrooms in the forest, she stumbled upon Mya, a young woman with a twisted ankle. Reluctantly, Destiny helped her back to town. Grateful for the assistance, Mya insisted on visiting Destiny's cabin to repay her kindness.

Mya's visits became a regular occurrence, and despite Destiny's initial resistance, she began to open up. Mya's warmth and genuine friendship started to melt the icy walls Destiny had built around herself. This budding friendship mirrored the internal struggle of Sméagol and Gollum—the part of her that longed for connection and the part that resisted it out of fear and mistrust. As Ecclesiastes 4:9-10 says, "Two are better than one... If either of them falls down, one can help the other up."

Destiny often felt like Gollum, whose dual personality is poignantly captured in the line: "Nobody likes you. Master is my friend. Leave now and never come back." Gollum's internal struggle between Sméagol, who desired friendship, and Gollum, who embraced isolation and suspicion, mirrored Destiny's own battle between seeking connection and retreating into loneliness.

Gollum's Manipulation and Satan's Deception

Gollum tries to isolate Frodo from Sam by saying, "He wants it. He needs it. Sméagol sees it in his eyes. Very soon he will ask you for it. You will see. The Fat One will take it from you," he sowed seeds of doubt and mistrust. Similarly, Satan uses lies and deception to isolate believers from their support systems and God.

- Satan's Lies: "He was a murderer from the beginning, not holding to the truth, for there is no truth in him. When he lies, he speaks his native language, for he is a liar and the father of lies" (John 8:44).

- Isolation through Deception: Satan tells believers that they are alone and unloved, much like Gollum told Frodo that Sam wanted the Ring. "Be alert and of sober mind. Your enemy, the devil, prowls around like a roaring lion looking for someone to devour" (1 Peter 5:8).

Destiny's mind echoed similar thoughts, driven by her isolation: "Nobody cares about you. Why would anyone want to help you?" These lies kept her trapped in a cycle of self-doubt and fear, preventing her from reaching out and accepting the help and friendship she so desperately needed.

Transformation and Healing

Mya, learning of Clearwater's healing spring, persuaded Destiny to visit it. With great trepidation, Destiny agreed. They approached the spring, watching others step into the waters with hope in their eyes. Mya gently guided Destiny to the edge, encouraging her to plunge.

Destiny hesitated, her mind swirling with excuses. "What if it doesn't work?" she thought, much like the man at Bethesda who had resigned himself to his fate. But Mya's unwavering support gave her the courage to step forward.

As Destiny entered the spring, she felt a profound warmth and release. The bitterness and loneliness that had gripped her heart began to dissolve. She realized that the healing she sought was physical, emotional, and spiritual. Like the man at Bethesda, who, upon encountering Jesus, was told, "Get up! Pick up your mat and walk" (John 5:8), Destiny felt a command to rise from her past and move forward. Similarly, David wrote in Psalm 25:16, "Turn to me and be gracious to me, for I am lonely and afflicted."

A New Beginning

Emerging from the spring, Destiny was transformed. No longer a recluse, she returned to Clearwater as a renewed woman, ready to embrace life and the community around her. Her friendship with Mya blossomed, a testament to the healing power of companionship.

Destiny began to help others in town, sharing her story and encouraging those who felt isolated and hopeless. She told them about her journey from isolation to connection, from excuses to empowerment, and how the revolving doors of her life had finally stopped spinning, allowing her to step into a new chapter. Hebrews 10:24-25 reminds us, "And let us consider how we may spur one another on toward love and good deeds, not giving up meeting together, as some are in the habit of doing but encouraging one another."

Toxicity

No longer a recluse and fresh out of isolation, Destiny assumed life was beautiful and full of promise. She basked in the warmth of her newfound friendship with Mya, feeling the joy of connection she had missed for so long. However, life's revolving doors had one more turn for Destiny—one that would challenge her newly found sense of trust and companionship.

One day, seemingly out of nowhere, Mya's behavior changed. She became distant, her once warm and supportive demeanor turning cold and critical. Destiny, who had once felt the burden of isolation lift, was again battling the shadows of doubt and loneliness. The echoes of Gollum's voice returned, "We be nice to them if they be nice to us," reminding her of the conditional nature of some relationships.

Destiny noticed that Mya's trust in her had begun to waver. Mya's attitude mirrored Gollum's suspicion and paranoia: "It's still trying to cheat us, it's doing its best to get us to let our guard down." This shift felt like a betrayal, striking at the heart of Destiny's fear of abandonment and rejection. "And what has it got in its pocketses?" Gollum's voice seemed to whisper in her mind, questioning the sincerity of her friend's actions and words.

A Betrayal Unfolds

Destiny confronted Mya, hoping to understand the sudden change. Instead of reassurance, she faced accusations and mistrust. Mya's words cut deep, stirring the old wounds of isolation and the fear of being unwanted. Mya accused Destiny of things she hadn't done, and the trust they had built seemed to crumble overnight.

Destiny's internal struggle mirrored Gollum's tormented dialogue with himself: "We swears, to do what you wants. We swears. There's no promise you can keep." She felt torn between the desire to hold on to this friendship and the fear that it was slipping away, much like Sméagol's grip on his remaining humanity.

Mya's harsh words and cold demeanor made Destiny question everything. The words echoed in her mind, "They will cheat you, hurt you, lie," reminiscent of Gollum's attempts to isolate Frodo from Sam. Destiny felt as if like she was being driven back into the isolation she had fought so hard to escape. Like Gollum's obsession with the Ring, she realized that Mya's

69

changing behavior reflected deeper issues that Destiny couldn't control or fix.

Reflections and Revelation

One evening, as Destiny stood by the spring that had once symbolized hope and healing, she saw her reflection in the water. She thought of Gollum's reflection in the pool, a tortured soul struggling between the light and darkness within. "Master tricked us, false. We ought to strangle them in their sleep. No, no! Too risky," Gollum's words played in her mind, representing the tug-of-war between her desire to trust

Destiny then remembered the story of King Saul and David from the scriptures. Their relationship had started with great promise and mutual respect. David had soothed Saul with his music and fought valiantly for his king. However, as David's popularity grew, Saul's jealousy and paranoia took over, turning their relationship toxic. "Saul was very angry; this refrain displeased him greatly. 'They have credited David with tens of thousands,' he thought, 'but me with only thousands. What more can he get but the kingdom?'" (1 Samuel 18:8).

Just like Saul turned on David, Mya had turned on Destiny. Saul's jealousy led him to isolate David, pursuing him relentlessly out of fear and suspicion. Destiny realized that Mya's actions were driven by her own insecurities and fears, not by Destiny's fault. This understanding helped Destiny to see the situation more clearly.

Moving Forward

Armed with this new perspective, Destiny decided to confront the situation with grace and honesty. She approached Mya, not with accusations, but with a heart ready to understand and heal. "We need to talk," Destiny said, her voice steady but kind. "I feel like something has changed between us, and I want to understand why."

Mya initially resisted, but as Destiny spoke about her confusion and hurt feelings, Mya began to open up. She revealed her own struggles and fears, admitting that she had felt threatened by Destiny's growing confidence and independence. "I'm sorry," Mya said, tears welling up. "I didn't know how to handle it and took it out on you."

This moment of vulnerability she was allowed them to mend their friendship. They discussed their insecurities and fears, realizing they had both been trapped in a cycle of mistrust and misunderstanding. As Ephesians 4:2-3 reminds us, "Be completely humble and gentle; be patient, bearing with one another in love. Make every effort to keep the unity of the Spirit through the bond of peace."

A Renewed Friendship

Destiny and Mya's friendship emerged stronger from this ordeal. They learned the importance of open communication and the dangers of letting fear and insecurity dictate their actions. Destiny understood that true healing and connection required vulnerability and honesty, much like the man at the Pool of Bethesda had to trust in Jesus' command to rise and walk.

Like the revolving doors of Destiny's life, their story had come full circle—from isolation to connection, from mistrust to understanding. They learned that while the doors of life might spin, it was possible to step through them with faith and courage, finding new beginnings and stronger bonds on the other side.

Destiny felt a renewed sense of purpose and hope as they continued their journey together. She knew challenges would still come, but she was no longer alone. She had Mya, her community, and her faith to guide her. And just as Frodo and Sam persevered against all odds, so too would Destiny and Mya, forging a path of love, trust, and resilience.

The Cycle Continues

However, life's revolving doors had another turn in store for Destiny. As she began sharing her dreams and the vision the Lord had placed on her heart, things turned dark. Instead of celebrating with her, Mya's betrayal deepened.

Destiny's dreams were grand and filled with hope. She envisioned a community center that would provide support and resources for those in need, inspired by her own journey from isolation to healing. She wanted to create a space where people could find connection, encouragement, and hope, much like she had found through her friendship with Mya and her faith.

But as Destiny shared her dreams, Mya's support waned. Instead of encouragement, Mya responded with skepticism and criticism. She questioned Destiny's ability to bring her vision to life, sowing doubt and discouragement. This betrayal cut deep, reminding Destiny of the story of Joseph and his brothers in the book of Genesis.

The Story of Joseph

Joseph was a dreamer, much like Destiny. He had visions of greatness, which he eagerly shared with his brothers. However, his brothers were consumed with jealousy and hatred instead of celebrating his dreams. "Here comes that dreamer!" they said to each other. "Come now, let's kill him and throw him into one of these cisterns and say that a ferocious animal devoured him. Then we'll see what comes of his dreams" (Genesis 37:19-20).

Just as Joseph's brothers betrayed him, Mya's betrayal left Destiny feeling isolated and alone again. Joseph's brothers sold him into slavery, and he was taken to Egypt, far from his home and family. Despite his circumstances, Joseph remained faithful to God, and his dreams came to pass in time. "You intended to harm me, but God intended it for good to accomplish what is now being done, saving many lives" (Genesis 50:20).

Reflections and Revelation

Destiny stood by the spring once more, reflecting on her journey. She realized that, like Joseph, she was facing betrayal and isolation. But she also knew that God had a plan for her that would bring her dreams to fruition despite the obstacles in her path. She remembered Romans 8:28, "And we know that in all things God works for the good of those who love him, who have been called according to his purpose."

Destiny decided to press on with her vision, trusting that God would guide her steps and provide the support she needed. She sought out others in the community who shared her passion and began to build a team of like-minded individuals who believed in her dream.

Be Careful Who You Share Your Vision With

During her trials, Destiny learned a valuable lesson: to be careful who you share your vision with. She recalled the words of Paul in Galatians 1:10, "Am I now trying to win the approval of human beings, or God? Or am I trying to please people? If I were still trying to please people, I would not be a servant of Christ." Destiny realized that seeking validation from others, especially those who harbor jealousy or insecurity, could lead to disappointment and betrayal.

Jesus Himself warned about this in Matthew 7:6, "Do not give dogs what is sacred; do not throw your pearls to pigs. If you do, they may trample them under their feet and turn and tear you to pieces." Destiny understood that her vision was precious, a sacred calling from God, and she needed to discern who she entrusted with her dreams.

Press On Anyway

Despite the betrayal and discouragement, Destiny chose to press on. She found strength in Philippians 3:13-14, "But one thing I do: Forgetting what is behind and straining toward what is ahead, I press on toward the goal to win the prize for which God has called me heavenward in Christ Jesus." Destiny knew that her journey was far from over, and she was determined to keep moving forward, trusting in God's plan and provision.

She found solace in the words of Isaiah 40:31, "But those who hope in the Lord will renew their strength. They will soar on wings like eagles; they will run and not grow weary; they will walk and not be faint." This promise gave her the courage to continue, knowing that God would sustain her through every challenge.

The Story of Samson and Delilah

Destiny's relationship with Mya took a turn for the worse as she reflected on the biblical story of Samson and Delilah—a narrative of trust, betrayal, and the consequences of toxic relationships. She started to see how Mya's betrayal could derail her dreams and visions, much like Samson's downfall, precipitated by his misplaced trust in Delilah.

Samson, a judge of Israel, was endowed with immense strength from God, symbolized by his uncut hair. Despite his divine calling, Samson's weakness for women led him into a relationship with Delilah, a Philistine woman who ultimately betrayed him. The Philistine rulers bribed Delilah to discover the secret of Samson's strength. Delilah's persistent questioning and manipulation finally wore Samson down, leading to his capture and downfall.

Judges 16:15-17 (NIV) narrates Delilah's relentless pursuit of Samson's secret:

"Then she said to him, 'How can you say, "I love you," when you won't confide in me? This is the third time you have made a fool of me and haven't told me the secret of your great strength.' With such nagging, she prodded him day after day until he was sick to death of it. So he told her everything. 'No razor has ever been used on my head,' he said, 'because I have been a Nazirite dedicated to God from my mother's womb. If my head were shaved, my strength would leave me, and I would become as weak as any other man.'"

Delilah's betrayal led to Samson's capture, his eyes being gouged out, and his eventual death. Samson's tragic end directly resulted from placing his trust in someone who sought his harm rather than his good.

Trust and Betrayal

Destiny, like Samson, placed her trust in Mya, sharing her dreams and visions openly. She believed that Mya, her friend, would support and encourage her. However, Mya's growing insecurity and jealousy turned her against Destiny. Instead of being a confidante, Mya became a source of discouragement and betrayal. This betrayal is similar to how Delilah betrayed Samson for personal gain, showing the devastating impact of misplaced trust.

Proverbs 27:6 (NIV): "Wounds from a friend can be trusted, but an enemy multiplies kisses."

This scripture highlights the pain of betrayal from someone close, a wound that cuts deeper than any inflicted by a known enemy.

Manipulation and Control

Mya's manipulation and discouraging words were like Delilah's persistent nagging and deceit. Delilah used her influence over Samson to manipulate him into revealing his secret. Similarly, Mya used her relationship with Destiny to sow seeds of doubt and hinder her from pursuing her God-given vision.

Proverbs 16:28 (NIV): "A perverse person stirs up conflict, and a gossip separates close friends."

This verse underscores how manipulative actions can destroy even the closest relationships, turning friends into adversaries.

Consequences of Betrayal

Samson's betrayal by Delilah led to his physical and spiritual downfall. Destiny's betrayal by Mya caused her emotional and spiritual turmoil, threatening to derail her vision and purpose. However, unlike Samson, Destiny chose to rise above the betrayal, seeking God's strength to press on with her mission.

1 Peter 5:8 (NIV): "Be alert and of sober mind. Your enemy, the devil, prowls around like a roaring lion looking for someone to devour."

This scripture serves as a reminder of the constant spiritual battle and the need for vigilance against those who might seek to derail us from our God-given path.

A Renewed Purpose

Despite Mya's betrayal, Destiny's faith remained unshaken. She understood that life's revolving doors might continue to spin, bringing challenges and betrayals, but she was determined to hold on to her vision. She leaned on scriptures that spoke of perseverance and faith, such as Philippians 4:13, "I can do all this through him who gives me strength," and Hebrews 11:1, "Now faith is confidence in what we hope for and assurance about what we do not see."

Destiny continued to share her vision with those who supported her and were aligned with her mission. She built a network of faithful friends and collaborators who believed in her dream and were committed to helping her bring it to life.

The Cycle Continues: Toxicity Comes To Its Conclusion

Destiny stood by the spring once more, reflecting on her journey. She realized that, like Joseph, she was facing betrayal and isolation. But she also knew that God had a plan for her that would bring her dreams to fruition despite the obstacles in her path. She remembered Romans 8:28, "And we know that in all things God works for the good of those who love him, who have been called according to his purpose."

As Destiny looked over the horizon, she saw Gollum standing by the edge of the water, his eyes reflecting a mix of longing and bitterness. His presence reminded her of the dangers of isolation and mistrust, of the voices that whispered doubt and fear. Yet, Gollum also reminded her of the frailty of the human heart, susceptible to greed and deception.

Beside Gollum stood the man at the pool of Bethesda, still waiting for someone to help him into the healing waters. His story echoed in Destiny's heart, a testament to the longing for change and the struggle against physical and emotional isolation.

And then there was Mya, once a friend whose betrayal had cut deep. Destiny gazed at Mya, seeing beyond the hurt and disappointment to the wounded soul within. She remembered the words of Jesus in Matthew 6:14, "For if you forgive other people when they sin against you, your heavenly Father will also forgive you."

Destiny realized that forgiveness was the key to breaking the cycle of toxicity. Just as Jesus had shown mercy and grace to those broken and lost, she knew she had to extend the same to Mya. It wasn't about excusing the betrayal but releasing herself from the chains of bitterness and resentment.

"Mya," Destiny spoke softly, her voice carrying the weight of both pain and compassion. "I forgive you. I release you from the hurt you caused me."

Mya looked up, surprise and remorse mingling in her eyes. "Destiny, I... I'm so sorry. I didn't mean to hurt you. I was... I was afraid."

Destiny nodded, tears welling in her eyes. "I understand. But we can't let fear and mistrust control us. We need to choose forgiveness and move forward."

Gollum shuffled closer, his gaze shifting between Destiny and Mya. "Forgiveness? Yes, precious. It's the only way to heal the wounds."

The man at the pool of Bethesda nodded in agreement, a flicker of hope lighting his weary eyes.

Destiny took Mya's hand, their fingers intertwining in a gesture of reconciliation. "Let's break this cycle together. Let's trust again, support each other's dreams, and walk in forgiveness."

As they stood by the spring, a sense of peace settled over them—a peace that transcended the hurts of the past and paved the way for a future filled with healing and restoration.

Destiny's journey through the revolving doors of life had taught her valuable lessons about trust, betrayal, and forgiveness. She had encountered characters like Gollum and the man at the pool of Bethesda, each reflecting aspects of her own struggles and victories. Through it all, Destiny had discovered the power of faith and resilience, anchored in her trust in God's plan for her life.

As she walked away from the spring with Mya by her side, Destiny knew their friendship had been tested and refined. They had weathered the storm of toxicity and emerged stronger, their bond forged in the fires of adversity. Destiny's vision for the community center remained alive and vibrant, fueled by her renewed faith and the support of true friends.

Destiny's revolving doors continued spinning, but she faced them with courage and hope. She knew that each turn brought new opportunities for growth and transformation. And as she looked ahead, Destiny embraced the future with a heart full of gratitude and a spirit ready to soar, guided by the love and grace that had carried her through it all.

In this conclusion, Destiny's story reflects the journey of overcoming betrayal and toxicity through forgiveness and faith, drawing parallels with biblical characters like Joseph, Samson, and the teachings of Jesus. It underscores the importance of trust, resilience, and the transformative power of forgiveness in relationships.

More Will Be Revealed: The Revolving Doors Continue

Chapter 5

Revolving Doors Part Two

I Can't Carry It For You... But I can carry you."

A revolving door typically means a door consisting of several horizontal panels rotating around a vertical axis within a cylindrical enclosure. It's often used at building entrances to control the flow of people entering and exiting while minimizing drafts and noise. Metaphorically, it can represent a situation with a constant turnover cycle, such as in employment or relationships. In relationships, a revolving door could describe a pattern where individuals repeatedly enter and exit relationships with different partners. It suggests a cycle of starting new relationships, encountering challenges or conflicts, and ending the relationship only to repeat the process with someone new.

Samwise Gamgee speaks that line to Frodo Baggins in J.R.R. Tolkien's "The Lord of the Rings: The Return of the King." It's a powerful moment near the end of their journey to destroy the One Ring. Frodo, burdened by the weight of the Ring and weakened by its influence, feels he can't go on. But Sam reassures him that while he can't carry the Ring for him, he can carry Frodo himself, both physically and emotionally. It's a testament to the strength of their friendship and Sam's unwavering loyalty.

I Can't Carry It For You... But I can carry you."

The Return of the King - "I Can't Carry It For You... But I can carry you."

"The Return of the King" is the final book in J.R.R. Tolkien's epic fantasy trilogy, "The Lord of the Rings." In this installment, the War of the Ring climaxes as the forces of good, led by the Free Peoples of Middle-earth, confront the dark lord Sauron and his army of orcs and allies in the land of Mordor.

The story picks up with Frodo Baggins and his loyal companion, Samwise Gamgee, continuing their perilous journey to Mount Doom in Mordor, where they aim to destroy the One Ring and thwart Sauron's plans for domination. Along the way, they face numerous trials and challenges, including encounters with the treacherous Gollum, who covets the Ring for himself.

Meanwhile, the rest of the Fellowship of the Ring, including Aragorn, Gandalf, Legolas, Gimli, Merry, and Pippin, rally the forces of men, elves, dwarves, and other allies to confront Sauron's armies in a final, desperate battle for the fate of Middle-earth.

As Frodo and Sam draw closer to Mount Doom, Frodo becomes increasingly burdened by the corrupting influence of the Ring, and Sam must carry him both physically and emotionally. In one of the story's most memorable moments, when Frodo feels he can no longer continue, Sam encourages him with the words, "I can't carry it for you, but I can carry you."

Ultimately, Frodo and Sam reach Mount Doom, where Frodo succumbs to the Ring's power and claims it himself. However, at the last moment, Gollum intervenes and bites off Frodo's finger, taking the Ring himself. In his ecstasy, Gollum falls into Mount Doom's fiery chasm, destroying himself and the Ring.

With the destruction of the Ring, Sauron is defeated, and his armies are vanquished. The Free Peoples of Middle-earth emerge victorious, but not without great sacrifice. The story ends with the hobbits returning to the Shire, only to find it changed by the war. Through their bravery and sacrifice, Frodo and Sam have saved Middle-earth from darkness, but their journey has taken a heavy toll on them and their homeland.

Revolving Door Relationship

In a revolving door relationship, there's a sense of cyclical behavior where individuals repeatedly enter and exit each other's lives, often encountering similar challenges or issues each time they reconnect.

The quote "I can't carry it for you, but I can carry you" from "The Return of the King" can relate to a revolving door relationship in the sense that one person may feel burdened by certain challenges or issues that arise each time they reunite with their partner. Just as Frodo feels overwhelmed by the burden of carrying the Ring, individuals in a revolving-door relationship may feel weighed down by unresolved issues or patterns that keep repeating.

Similarly, just as Sam offers support and reassurance to Frodo, individuals in a revolving door relationship may offer emotional support and assistance to each other, even though they may not fully resolve the underlying issues causing the relationship to cycle.

The quote highlights the idea of offering support and companionship in the face of ongoing challenges, even if the underlying problems cannot be fully resolved. In a revolving door relationship, this support can be crucial in navigating the repeated cycles and maintaining a sense of connection despite the challenges.

Let us look at the parallel between the story of the Lord of the Rings, The quote "I can't carry it for you, but I can carry you" from "The Return of the King," and the story found in Luke 5:17-26.

Luke 5:17-26 NLV On one of the days, while Jesus was teaching, some proud religious law-keepers and teachers of the Law were sitting by Him. They had come from every town in the countries of Galilee and, Judea, and from Jerusalem. The power of the Lord was there to heal them. 18 Some men took a man who was not able to move his body to Jesus. He was carried on a bed. They looked for a way to take the man into the house where Jesus was. 19 But they could not find a way to take him in because of so many people. They made a hole in the roof over where Jesus stood. Then they let the bed with the sick man on it down before Jesus. 20 When Jesus saw their faith, He said to the man, "Friend, your sins are forgiven." 21 The Pharisees and the teachers of the law began thinking to themselves, "Who is this fellow who speaks blasphemy? Who can forgive sins but God alone?"

22 Jesus knew what they were thinking and asked, "Why are you thinking these things in your hearts? 23 Which is easier: to say, 'Your sins are forgiven,' or to say, 'Get up and walk'? 24 But I want you to know that the Son of Man has authority on earth to forgive sins." So he said to the paralyzed man, "I tell you, get up, take your mat, and go home." 25 Immediately he stood up in front of them, took what he had been lying on and went home praising God. 26 Everyone was amazed and gave praise to God. They were filled with awe and said, "We have seen remarkable things today.

In "The Lord of the Rings," Sam's profound declaration to Frodo, "I can't carry it for you, but I can carry you," encapsulates the essence of sacrificial friendship amidst monumental challenges. Sam's loyalty and steadfastness serve as a beacon of hope for Frodo as they journey through the perils of Middle-earth. Sam's presence provides physical aid and emotional fortitude, reminding Frodo that he is not alone in his struggle against the darkness of the Ring.

Similarly, in the account of Luke, the friends of the paralyzed man demonstrate remarkable faith and determination by going to great lengths to bring their companion to Jesus for healing. Despite encountering obstacles, they refuse to be deterred, showcasing the transformative power of steadfast support and unwavering belief. Their collective efforts lead to physical healing and result in the forgiveness of sins, highlighting the profound impact of communal faith and solidarity.

Both narratives show the importance of surrounding oneself with supportive companions. These stories underscore the invaluable role of companionship in times of adversity, emphasizing the need for individuals to cultivate relationships built on trust, empathy, and mutual encouragement. Just as Frodo finds strength in Sam's unwavering loyalty and the paralyzed man experiences healing through the faith of his friends, we are reminded of the transformative power of genuine connections.

Ultimately, these narratives serve as poignant reminders of the inherent human need for community and the profound impact of surrounding oneself with those who will uplift support, and journey alongside us through life's trials and tribulations. In times of darkness and uncertainty, we find solace, strength, and the courage to persevere through the bonds of friendship and faith.

In the context of a revolving door relationship, the parallels between these narratives and the necessity of surrounding oneself with supportive companions have added significance.

A revolving door relationship is characterized by cycles of separation and reunion, often accompanied by recurring challenges or issues. In such dynamics, individuals may find themselves repeatedly navigating familiar obstacles, unable to break free from patterns of conflict or instability.

Drawing from the narratives of "The Lord of the Rings" and the story from Luke, we can discern valuable insights into addressing the complexities of a revolving door relationship. Just as Frodo finds solace in Sam's unwavering support and the paralyzed man experiences healing through the collective faith of his friends, individuals in revolving-door relationships must seek out and cultivate supportive connections.

These supportive companions serve as anchors amidst the turbulence of the relationship, offering guidance, empathy, and encouragement during times of struggle. They provide a sense of stability and reassurance, empowering individuals to confront recurring challenges with resilience and determination.

Moreover, the narratives highlight the transformative power of communal faith and solidarity. In a revolving door relationship, individuals can draw strength from the shared belief in the possibility of positive change and growth. Through collective efforts and mutual support, they can navigate the cycles of separation and reunion with a renewed sense of hope and purpose.

Ultimately, the parallels between these narratives and the dynamics of a revolving door relationship underscore the importance of fostering supportive connections and nurturing faith in the possibility of transformation. By surrounding oneself with companions who offer unwavering support and shared belief, individuals can navigate the complexities of their relationship journey with greater resilience, courage, and grace. Let us transition our focus to the story of a man named Dakota from Carson City, Nevada. Let us transition our focus to the story of a man named Dakota from Carson City, Nevada.

Title: "I Can't Carry It For You... But I Can Carry You"

In the small town of Carson City, Nevada, lived a young man named Dakota. He was known for his kind heart and unwavering determination, but his life seemed stuck in a relentless cycle of highs and lows—a revolving door of relationships and challenges he couldn't quite escape.

Dakota's most significant struggle was his on-again, off-again relationship with his childhood friend, Ayasha. They had been through thick and thin together, but recurring conflicts and separations marked their relationship. Despite their love for each other, they couldn't break free from the patterns pulling them apart.

One day, as Dakota sat on the porch of his modest home, feeling the weight of his latest separation from Ayasha, his best friend, Elan, arrived. Elan had been by Dakota's side since they were kids, and his loyalty never wavered. He reminded Dakota of Samwise Gamgee from "The Lord of the Rings," always there to support him, no matter how heavy the burden.

"Dakota, I know things are tough right now," Elan said, sitting beside him. "But remember what Sam told Frodo: 'I can't carry it for you, but I can carry you.' You don't have to go through this alone."

Dakota looked at Elan, feeling a flicker of hope. He knew that Elan's words were more than just a quote from a beloved book; they were a testament to the power of friendship and loyalty.

As they talked, Elan reminded Dakota of another story that had always inspired them both. He recounted the tale from Luke 5:17-26, where a group of friends went to extraordinary lengths to bring their paralyzed companion to Jesus for healing. Despite the obstacles, they persisted, lowering their friend through the roof to ensure he received the needed help.

"Dakota," Elan continued, "just like those friends who believed in the power of healing and refused to give up, we need to have faith and keep pushing forward. You've got people who care about you, who believe in you. We'll get through this together."

With Elan's support, Dakota began to see his situation differently. He realized that, like Frodo and the paralyzed man, he didn't have to bear his burdens alone. The strength and faith of those around him could help him navigate the revolving door of his relationship with Ayasha and the challenges in his life.

Elan also shared with Dakota some other scriptures that spoke to the power of friendship and support:

Proverbs 17:17: "A friend loves at all times, and a brother is born for a time of adversity." This verse reminded Dakota that true friends are always there, especially in difficult times.

Ecclesiastes 4:9-10: "Two are better than one, because they have a good return for their labor: If either of them falls down, one can help the other up. But pity anyone who falls and has no one to help them up." This scripture emphasized the importance of companionship and mutual support.

John 15:12-13: "My command is this: Love each other as I have loved you. Greater love has no one than this: to lay down one's life for one's friends." These words of Jesus highlighted the depth of true friendship and the willingness to support and sacrifice for one another.

As the weeks passed, Dakota leaned on Elan and his other friends more than ever. They provided the stability and encouragement he needed to face his fears and work on his relationship with Ayasha. Through open communication and mutual support, Dakota and Ayasha began to break the cycle that had trapped them for so long.

Dakota understood the profound truth in Sam's words and Luke's story in time. Loyal friends, like Elan, could not carry his burdens for him, but their unwavering support and faith could carry him through the toughest times. Together, they helped him find the strength to heal, grow, and move forward.

Dakota's journey was far from over, but he now knew he wasn't alone. With loyal friends by his side and the wisdom of scripture guiding him, he could face any challenge and navigate the revolving doors of life with hope and resilience.

Who Can Find One Faithful: The Need for Accountability

Dakota's journey in Carson City wasn't just about navigating the highs and lows of his relationship with Ayasha. It was also about understanding the importance of true friendship and the role of accountability in fostering positive, enduring connections. As he reflected on his life, Dakota realized the significance of Proverbs 20:6: "Many claim to have unfailing love, but a faithful person who can find?"

Elan, Dakota's steadfast friend, embodied the essence of this proverb. His unwavering loyalty and dedication reminded Dakota of the value of having someone reliable. Elan wasn't just a friend who offered support; he also held Dakota accountable, challenging him to grow and face his issues head-on.

To illustrate this, Elan shared another piece of wisdom from the scriptures:

Proverbs 27:17: "As iron sharpens iron, so one person sharpens another." This verse emphasizes the role of friends in refining each other, much like how Elan's presence helped Dakota become a better person.

Elan encouraged Dakota to embrace accountability as a cornerstone of their friendship. He explained that true friends don't just offer comfort but also challenge each other to live with integrity and purpose. This mutual accountability was essential for navigating the revolving doors of their friendship, ensuring that they supported each other through life's cycles of change.

Elan also shared a passage from Galatians that highlighted the importance of bearing each other's burdens:

Galatians 6:2: "Carry each other's burdens, and in this way, you will fulfill the law of Christ." This scripture reminded Dakota that accountability was about sharing the load, much like how Elan had been carrying him through tough times and how he was expected to do the same for others.

Dakota began to see the value in fostering accountability within his broader circle of friends. He understood that positive revolving doors in relationships—those cycles of separation and reunion—could be strengthened through mutual support and accountability. These friendships could endure and thrive by holding each other to higher standards and encouraging growth.

Another scripture that resonated with Dakota was from Hebrews:

Hebrews 10:24-25: "And let us consider how we may spur one another on toward love and good deeds, not giving up meeting together, as some are in the habit of doing, but encouraging one another—and all the more as you see the Day approaching." This passage reinforced the idea that continuous engagement and encouragement were vital for maintaining strong, accountable relationships.

In his journey, Dakota also drew inspiration from Ecclesiastes, which emphasized the strength found in unity:

Ecclesiastes 4:12: "Though one may be overpowered, two can defend themselves. A cord of three strands is not quickly broken." This verse underscored the importance of a strong support network, where friends stand together and uphold each other through accountability and shared strength.

With these scriptures as his guide, Dakota embraced the need for faithful and accountable friends in his life. He sought to build and nurture relationships where mutual support and accountability were paramount, ensuring that the revolving doors of his friendships were not sources of instability but rather opportunities for growth and deeper connection.

In the end, Dakota learned that while he couldn't carry the burdens of life alone, he could rely on his friends to carry him when needed, just as he would carry them. Together, they formed a resilient community of faithful individuals who sharpened each other, bore each other's burdens, and spurred one another toward love and good deeds. This was the essence of true friendship and the key to navigating the revolving doors of life.

From my own personal journey

I recalled the time when he decided that if I was going to embrace this Christian journey, I couldn't do it alone. Attending church was a good start, but he often found something missing. Walking through the church doors, exchanging pleasantries like "How's it going today?" and "What's up, brother or sister?" often felt superficial. Despite saying things like "I'm blessed, blessed and highly favored, praise God for being here today," I still carried heavy burdens.

I longed for deeper connections where I could truly open up about what was happening in my life. I needed someone to rely on, to trust, and to confide in—someone who could offer wisdom, direction, counsel, comfort, and even correction. Those I had left behind couldn't fulfill my desire for change.

Then, one day, I was introduced to a group of men who met at 5:00 AM on Thursday mornings, holding each other to a higher standard of living. This group was exactly what I needed—no more drive-by services or faking it until making it. Here, I could be just Darick, with all my junk in the trunk, supported by brothers who would help me walk the Christian life the right way.

These men were far from perfect, but we were willing to hold each other to the standards of being Faithful, Accountable, and Teachable (F.A.T.). They couldn't carry my burdens for me, but they were willing to carry me through the journey, much like the friends of the paralyzed man who went to great lengths to bring their friend to Jesus.

My journey with this group of men began in 2002, and 22 years later, many of these same brothers are still deeply rooted in my life. They had become my Samwise Gamgees, my companions who helped me navigate the revolving doors of life with hope and resilience.

Reflecting on my own experience, I realized how much my story paralleled the narratives of "The Lord of the Rings" and the paralyzed man in Luke 5:17-26. I continue to see the importance of surrounding myself with loyal friends who offer support, accountability, and unwavering faith.

A Friend That Sticks Closer Than a Brother.

Ultimately, Dakota's story highlighted the profound truth that while no one could carry his burdens for him, having faithful friends by his side to carry him through tough times made all the difference. With their support and the wisdom of scripture, Dakota found the strength to face life's challenges and navigate the revolving doors of his relationships with faith, hope, and resilience.

Dakota longed for new, loyal friends to walk with him on his journey. He desired friendships rooted in trust, accountability, and mutual support—friendships that reflected the wisdom of Proverbs 18:24: "One who has unreliable friends soon comes to ruin, but there is a friend who sticks closer than a brother."

In his quest for such companionship, Dakota met Jamal. Jamal was new to Carson City, having moved from a bustling metropolis in search of a quieter life. He was a man of strong faith and shared Dakota's desire for genuine, supportive relationships.

From the moment they met, Dakota and Jamal clicked. Jamal's kindness, integrity, and unwavering faith reminded Dakota of Elan, his steadfast friend. Jamal quickly became a pivotal part of Dakota's support network, embodying the essence of a friend who sticks closer than a brother.

Their friendship grew as they spent time together, sharing their struggles, hopes, and dreams. Jamal often reminded Dakota of another powerful scripture:

Proverbs 27:9"Perfume and incense bring joy to the heart, and the pleasantness of a friend springs from their heartfelt advice." This verse underscored the joy and comfort of genuine friendship, much like the connection between Dakota and Jamal.

Jamal was not just a confidant; he was also an accountability partner. He held Dakota to high standards, encouraging him to grow in his faith and personal life. He challenged Dakota to be honest with himself and others, seek wisdom, and embrace their faith community's support.

Together, they leaned on scriptures that spoke to the power of mutual support and accountability:

James 5:16: "Therefore confess your sins to each other and pray for each other so that you may be healed. The prayer of a righteous person is powerful and effective." This verse highlighted the importance of transparency and prayer in their friendship, fostering a deep sense of trust and healing.

1 Thessalonians 5:11: "Therefore encourage one another and build each other up, just as in fact you are doing." Jamal and Dakota took this scripture to heart, consistently encouraging and uplifting one another in their daily lives.

As Dakota continued his journey, he saw how his friendship with Jamal mirrored the story of Samwise Gamgee and Frodo in "The Lord of the Rings." Just as Sam refused to leave Frodo's side and carried him when he could go no further, Jamal stood by Dakota through every trial, offering unwavering support and strength.

Their bond also reflected the story from Luke 5:17-26, where friends went to extraordinary lengths to bring their paralyzed companion to Jesus. Jamal's commitment to Dakota's well-being was a testament to the power of loyal, faithful friendship—a friendship that would go to any length to provide support and healing.

Over time, Dakota's circle of support grew to include other like-minded individuals who shared his values and faith. Together, they formed a tight-knit community where everyone held each other accountable, inspired one another to grow, and provided a safe space for sharing their burdens.

Dakota's journey taught him that true friendship, rooted in faith and accountability, was essential for navigating the revolving doors of life. He learned that while unreliable friends could lead to ruin, a friend who sticks closer than a brother could provide the strength and support needed to overcome any challenge.

Dakota faced life's ups and downs with renewed hope and resilience with Jamal and his other loyal friends by his side. He no longer felt alone in his struggles, knowing that he had a steadfast support network to carry him through. This powerful realization deepened his faith and commitment to fostering genuine, accountable relationships, allowing him to navigate the revolving doors of life with confidence and grace.

Formation of Their Friendship

Not long after forming a bond with Jamal, Dakota met another friend who would become a cornerstone in his life— Chayton. Their friendship quickly blossomed, reminding Dakota of the deep and loyal bond between David and Jonathan from the Bible.

Reflecting on the story of David and Jonathan, Dakota recalled the key moments that defined their friendship:

1 Samuel 18:1-4: After David defeated Goliath, Jonathan, King Saul's son, formed an immediate bond with David. They

made a covenant, signifying a deep and lasting friendship. Jonathan gave David his robe, armor, sword, bow, and belt, symbolizing his commitment and support.

Chayton, like Jonathan, showed his loyalty to Dakota in profound ways. He always offered support, encouragement, and a listening ear. Their friendship was grounded in mutual respect and an unwavering commitment to each other's well-being.

Loyalty and Protection

Just as Jonathan protected David from King Saul's jealousy, Chayton stood by Dakota during his most challenging times.

1 Samuel 19:1-7: When King Saul sought to kill David out of jealousy, Jonathan warned David and interceded on his behalf. Jonathan spoke well of David to Saul, convincing his father to spare David's life temporarily.

Chayton often intervened when Dakota faced personal struggles, offering wisdom and guidance to help him navigate difficult situations. His loyalty was a source of strength for Dakota, much like Jonathan's loyalty was for David.

Renewal of Covenant

Their bond deepened as they faced life's challenges together, reaffirming their commitment to each other:

1 Samuel 20: David sought Jonathan's help to confirm Saul's intentions. They devised a plan involving arrows to communicate Saul's intent. Jonathan reaffirmed his loyalty and love for David, even though it risked his own standing with his father.

Dakota and Chayton often had heart-to-heart conversations, discussing their dreams, fears, and faith. They consciously supported each other, renewing their commitment to be there for one another through thick and thin.

Final Meeting

There were moments when Dakota faced his greatest challenges, and Chayton was there to encourage him:

1 Samuel 23:16-18: Jonathan visited David in Horesh despite the dangers. He encouraged David, affirming that he would be king and that Jonathan would support him. They renewed their covenant before the Lord.

Chayton's visits to Dakota during tough times were like Jonathan's visits to David. He encouraged and reminded Dakota of God's promises, helping him find strength in his faith and purpose.

Accountability in Their Relationship

Their friendship was marked by honesty, moral support, and a willingness to rebuke wrong intentions:

Honesty: Jonathan was honest with David about the dangers he faced from Saul, and David trusted Jonathan to relay the truth, even when it was hard. This mutual honesty was crucial for their safety and plans.

Chayton and Dakota shared a similar level of honesty, always being truthful with each other, even when the truth was difficult to hear. This honesty was foundational for their trust and accountability.

Moral Support: Jonathan consistently supported David, reminding him of God's promises and encouraging him to stay strong in faith and purpose. For example, when Jonathan visited David at Horesh, he helped him find strength in God"(1 Samuel 23:16).

Chayton played a similar role in Dakota's life, constantly reminding him of God's faithfulness and encouraging him to pursue his calling with confidence and hope.

Rebuking Wrong Intentions: Jonathan didn't hesitate to confront his father, Saul, about his unjust actions toward David. He argued that David had not wronged Saul and that his actions were evil (1 Samuel 19:4-5). This shows Jonathan's commitment to justice and righteousness, even against his own family.

Chayton wasn't afraid to call out Dakota when he saw him veering off course. He held Dakota accountable, challenging him to live with integrity and to align his actions with his faith.

The Need for Elevation

Chayton wasn't afraid to call out Dakota when he saw him veering off course. He held Dakota accountable, challenging him to live with integrity and to align his actions with his faith. This kind of friendship was invaluable, but Dakota knew that he needed a mentor and coach to elevate his spiritual walk.

As Dakota journeyed through these positive revolving door relationships, he realized he needed guidance from someone with more experience and wisdom. He prayed for a mentor and coach who could help him grow in his faith and provide the spiritual direction he craved. His prayers were answered when he was introduced to a gentleman named Jay Eclair.

Jay Eclair was a seasoned man of faith, known in the community for his deep understanding of scripture and his ability to guide others in their spiritual journeys. Dakota felt a strong connection with Jay from their first meeting, much like the biblical relationship between Elisha and Elijah.

Reflections on Elisha and Elijah

As their mentor-mentee relationship developed, Dakota often reflected on the story of Elisha and Elijah, drawing parallels to his own journey with Jay:

1. Calling and Commitment:

1 Kings 19:19-21: When Elijah called Elisha to follow him, Elisha demonstrated his commitment by leaving his family and livelihood. He slaughtered his oxen and burned his plowing equipment, symbolizing his complete dedication to God's call.

Dakota saw his decision to seek out Jay's mentorship as a similar act of commitment. He was ready to leave behind his old ways and fully embrace God's path for him, guided by Jay's wisdom.

2. Learning and Growth:

2 Kings 2:1-6: Elisha followed Elijah closely, learning from him and witnessing his miracles. Elisha's dedication to learning from Elijah showed his desire to grow and develop his faith.

Dakota eagerly soaked up Jay's teachings, asking questions and seeking advice on navigating life's challenges with a godly perspective. Jay's mentorship provided Dakota with the spiritual nourishment he needed to grow.

3. Receiving the Mantle:

2 Kings 2:7-15: Before Elijah was taken up to heaven, Elisha asked for a double portion of Elijah's spirit. When Elijah was taken up in a whirlwind, Elisha picked up Elijah's cloak, symbolizing the passing of the prophetic mantle and the continuation of Elijah's ministry.

Jay often reminded Dakota that true growth in faith comes from God and that his role was to guide Dakota toward that divine empowerment. Dakota felt a sense of spiritual elevation, knowing that with Jay's mentorship, he was prepared to carry forward his ministry and purpose.

4. Performing Miracles:

2 Kings 2:19-22: After receiving Elijah's mantle, Elisha began performing miracles, demonstrating that he had inherited Elijah's prophetic power.

With Jay's guidance, Dakota began to see tangible changes in his life. He found himself more confident in his faith, more effective in his ministry, and more capable of handling life's challenges. Jay helped Dakota recognize his own potential and encouraged him to step into his God-given role.

Just as Dakota found himself needing a mentor, I, too, recognized that to elevate my spiritual journey, I needed guidance from someone wiser and more experienced. I prayed for a mentor and was blessed with one who helped me navigate my faith journey, much like Jay did for Dakota.

The Impact of Jay's Mentorship

Under Jay's mentorship, Dakota learned the importance of having a spiritual coach. Jay provided Dakota with practical advice, scriptural insights, and personal stories that illustrated the principles of faith. They often studied passages like:

Proverbs 27:17: "As iron sharpens iron, so one person sharpens another." Jay's mentorship sharpened Dakota's understanding of scripture and his application of faith in daily life.

2 Timothy 2:2: "And the things you have heard me say in the presence of many witnesses entrust to reliable people who will also be qualified to teach others." Jay taught Dakota the importance of passing on what he learned to others, fostering a culture of mentorship and growth.

Jay's influence was profound. He helped Dakota see beyond his current struggles and envision a future where he could mentor others. Jay's guidance illuminated the path for Dakota, showing him that true elevation in faith comes from a combination of personal devotion, community support, and wise mentorship.

Dakota's faith was elevated to new heights through these relationships and Jay's mentorship. He embraced his role as a mentor to others, just as Elisha continued Elijah's work. Dakota's growth, support, and elevation journey exemplify the power of faithful friendships and the transformative impact of spiritual mentorship.

Pass the Baton

He embraced his role as a mentor to others. Dakota knew that to continue growing, he would have to pour into someone else. He now ran into a young man named Ashkii, who inquired about learning from Dakota. Ashkii was wet behind the ears, but he showed great hunger and potential for learning. Dakota recognized that this relationship was like Paul and Timothy's.

Reflections on Paul and Timothy

As Dakota began mentoring Ashkii, he often reflected on the relationship between Paul and Timothy:

1. Selection and Encouragement:

Acts 16:1-3: Paul met Timothy in Lystra and saw his potential. Despite his youth, Paul chose Timothy to accompany him on his missionary journeys, encouraging him to grow in his faith and ministry.

Dakota saw the same potential in Ashkii. He knew that with the right guidance and encouragement, Ashkii could become a strong leader in the faith. Dakota began investing time in Ashkii, sharing his experiences, and teaching him the ways of the Lord.

2. Training and Discipleship:

2 Timothy 2:2: "And the things you have heard me say in the presence of many witnesses entrust to reliable people who will also be qualified to teach others." Paul emphasized the importance of passing on knowledge and training others to continue the work of the ministry.

Dakota embraced this principle wholeheartedly. He dedicated himself to teaching Ashkii the basics of the faith and the deeper truths and responsibilities of living a life devoted to God. Dakota taught Ashkii how to study the scriptures, pray earnestly, and live out his faith in practical ways.

3. Guidance and Correction:

1 Timothy 4:12: "Don't let anyone look down on you because you are young, but set an example for the believers in speech, in conduct, in love, in faith, and in purity." Paul guided Timothy, encouraging him to be an example despite his youth and to live a life of integrity.

Dakota provided similar guidance to Ashkii, helping him navigate the challenges of being a young believer. He corrected Ashkii with love when necessary and praised him when he saw growth and maturity. Dakota knew that true discipleship involved both encouragement and correction.

4. Empowerment and Commissioning:

2 Timothy 4:2: "Preach the word; be prepared in season and out of season; correct, rebuke and encourage—with great patience and careful instruction." Paul empowered Timothy to take on leadership roles and fulfill his ministry.

Dakota saw Ashkii's growth and began to empower him to take on more responsibilities. He encouraged Ashkii to share his faith, lead small groups, and eventually mentor others. Dakota's mentorship was about equipping Ashkii to become a mentor, continuing the discipleship cycle.

My Personal Journey

Reflecting on my own journey, I realized that, much like Dakota, I needed to pass on what I had learned. My early days in the Thursday morning group were formative, but I felt a calling to mentor others as I grew. I prayed for someone to pour into, and soon, I met men who reminded me of my younger self. I saw the same hunger and potential in them that someone saw in me.

Dakota Mentorship of Ashkii

Dakota and Ashkii's relationship flourished. They spent countless hours studying scripture, praying, and discussing life's challenges and triumphs. Dakota shared his own struggles and victories, providing Ashkii with a roadmap for navigating his faith journey.

Dakota often used Paul's letters to Timothy as a teaching tool, emphasizing the importance of:

Faithfulness: "Fight the good fight of the faith. Take hold of the eternal life to which you were called when you made your good confession in the presence of many witnesses" (1 Timothy 6:12).

Perseverance: "Endure hardship with us like a good soldier of Christ Jesus" (2 Timothy 2:3).

Integrity: "Keep yourself pure" (1 Timothy 5:22).

Ashkii thrived under Dakota's mentorship, growing in confidence and wisdom. Dakota encouraged Ashkii to step out in faith, take risks for the Gospel's sake, and always rely on God's strength.

Just as Jay had mentored Dakota, he now passed the baton to Ashkii. He understood that his role was not just to teach but to empower Ashkii to become a mentor to others. Dakota often reminded Ashkii of 2 Timothy 2:2, encouraging him to look for reliable people he could teach and train.

Dakota's journey from being mentored to mentoring others exemplifies the biblical principle of discipleship. By pouring into Ashkii, Dakota ensured the legacy of faith, accountability, and support would continue. Ashkii, like Timothy, was prepared to take on the leadership mantle and pass on what he had learned to future generations.

Dakota's faith was strengthened through these revolving door relationships, which enriched his life. He learned that true growth comes from receiving, giving, investing in others, and watching them flourish. This cycle of mentorship and discipleship created a strong, interconnected community of believers; each committed to helping the next person grow in their faith.

Seasoned Relationships: Everyone Is Not Meant to Stay

Each committed to helping the next person, creating a ripple effect of faith, accountability, and support. As Dakota watched Ashkii grow in his own role as a mentor, he felt a deep sense of fulfillment. Ashkii was excited about leading and coaching a new prospect named Eagle Eye. This new relationship reminded Dakota of the story of Paul, Barnabas, and John Mark.

Reflections on Paul, Barnabas, and John Mark

Dakota shared with Ashkii the lessons from the relationship between Paul, Barnabas, and John Mark, illustrating the importance of understanding that not all relationships are meant to last forever.

1. Initial Partnership and Disappointment:

Acts 13:5: John Mark initially accompanied Paul and Barnabas on their missionary journey. However, he left them early on, returning to Jerusalem (Acts 13:13). This caused disappointment, particularly for Paul.

Dakota emphasized to Ashkii that people sometimes start with enthusiasm but may not continue the journey for various reasons. Though eager now, Eagle Eye might face challenges that could lead him to step back.

2. Conflict and Separation:

Acts 15:36-39: Paul and Barnabas sharply disagreed about taking John Mark on their next journey. Barnabas wanted to give him another chance, while Paul did not. This disagreement led to Paul and Barnabas parting ways, with Barnabas taking John Mark and Paul choosing Silas.

Dakota highlighted the lesson that even strong partnerships can experience conflict and separation. He reminded Ashkii that disagreements are a part of life and ministry. Sometimes, it's necessary to part ways to pursue God's calling more effectively.

3. Redemption and Reconciliation:

2 Timothy 4:11: Later, Paul acknowledged John Mark's value, asking Timothy to bring him along because he was helpful in his ministry. This showed that relationships could be restored and people could grow and change.

Dakota encouraged Ashkii always to leave the door open for reconciliation. Even if Eagle Eye or others falter, there might be an opportunity for future collaboration and growth.

Ashkii and Eagle Eye's Journey

Ashkii approached his new role excitedly, ready to pour into Eagle Eye as Dakota had done for him. They met regularly, discussing scriptures, praying together, and exploring what it meant to live a life of faith. Ashkii was patient and understanding, aware that everyone's journey was unique.

Dakota observed their relationship and was ready to offer support and guidance. He saw the potential in Eagle Eye but also recognized the challenges ahead. Dakota shared the story of Paul, Barnabas, and John Mark with Ashkii, preparing him for the possibility that Eagle Eye's path might not align perfectly with theirs.

Dakota taught Ashkii the importance of recognizing the seasonal nature of some relationships. He shared:

Ecclesiastes 3:1: "There is a time for everything and a season for every activity under the heavens." Dakota emphasized that understanding the seasons in relationships helps to manage expectations and fosters growth, whether people stay or leave.

Proverbs 27:17: "As iron sharpens iron, so one person sharpens another." Dakota reminded Ashkii that even temporary relationships could provide valuable lessons and growth opportunities.

Personal Reflection

In my own life, I experienced similar transitions. Some people walked with me for a season, and others for a lifetime. The group of men I met at 5:00 AM on Thursdays taught me the value of deep, committed relationships. Yet, over time, some of those men moved on, and new ones emerged. Each relationship, whether brief or long-lasting, contributed to my growth.

Dakota's Continued Mentorship

Dakota continued to mentor Ashkii, helping him navigate the complexities of leadership and mentorship. He encouraged Ashkii to be patient with Eagle Eye, to invest in him fully, and to be prepared for the possibility that Eagle Eye might choose a different path.

Dakota also taught Ashkii to recognize and cherish those relationships that lasted. He reminded Ashkii that while some people are only in our lives for a season, they leave lasting impacts. Others stay, becoming lifelong friends and partners in faith.

Through his journey, Dakota learned that the essence of the revolving door of relationships is not just about who comes and goes but about the growth and impact that each interaction brings. Whether relationships are for a season or a lifetime, each one plays a crucial role in our spiritual development.

Intertwined with the biblical examples of Paul, Barnabas, John Mark, and the many mentors and mentees in his life, Dakota's story highlights the importance of faith, accountability, and the willingness to pour into others. By embracing these principles, Dakota created a legacy of mentorship and discipleship, ensuring that each person he mentored was equipped to do the same for others.

Ride or Die: Those who carry each other to the End.

Dakota created a legacy of mentorship and discipleship, ensuring that each person he mentored was equipped to do the same for others. Despite these fruitful relationships, Dakota longed for lasting friendships he could count on. He sought the Lord earnestly, praying for a companion who would be there through thick and thin. During this time, Dee Rock entered his life, a true "ride or die" friend, someone with whom he could share the journey to the very end.

A Bond Like Ruth and Naomi

As Dakota and Dee Rock's friendship grew, Dakota was reminded of the story of Ruth and Naomi. Their relationship embodied the unwavering loyalty and support that Dakota had always desired in a friendship.

1. Unwavering Loyalty:

-Ruth 1:16-17: "But Ruth replied, 'Don't urge me to leave you or to turn back from you. Where you go, I will go, and where you stay, I will stay. Your people will be my people and your God my God. Where you die I will die, and there I will be buried. May the Lord deal with me, be it ever so severely, if even death separates you and me.'"

Dakota saw this same unwavering loyalty in Dee Rock. From the moment they met, Dee Rock made it clear that he would stand by Dakota through any trial or triumph. They shared a commitment to each other and a deep faith in God that bound them together.

2. Support in Times of Hardship:

Ruth 2:11-12: Boaz replied, "I've been told all about what you have done for your mother-in-law since the death of your husband—how you left your father and mother and your homeland and came to live with a people you did not know before. May the Lord repay you for what you have done. May you be richly rewarded by the Lord, the God of Israel, under whose wings you have come to take refuge."

Just as Ruth supported Naomi through their difficult journey, Dee Rock stood by Dakota during his toughest times. Whether it was a personal crisis or a spiritual battle, Dee Rock provided the strength and encouragement Dakota needed.

3. Shared Faith and Purpose:

Ruth 4:14-15: "The women said to Naomi: 'Praise be to the Lord, who this day has not left you without a guardian-redeemer. May he become famous throughout Israel! He will renew your life and sustain you in your old age. For your daughter-in-law, who loves you and who is better to you than seven sons, has given him birth.'"

Their friendship was built on a shared faith and purpose. They encouraged each other to grow closer to God and to live out their faith in tangible ways. Dee Rock reminded Dakota that their journey was about personal growth and glorifying God through their lives and actions.

Dakota and Dee Rock's Journey

Together, Dakota and Dee Rock faced numerous challenges and celebrated many victories. Their friendship was marked by deep conversations, shared prayers, and a mutual commitment to each other's well-being. They held each other accountable, encouraged each other to pursue their God-given dreams, and supported each other through every trial.

Dakota often reflected on their friendship and how it paralleled the story of Ruth and Naomi. He was grateful for Dee Rock's loyalty and unwavering support. They both understood that their friendship was a gift from God, meant to help them navigate the ups and downs of life.

My Personal Journey

Reflecting on my own life, I saw a similar pattern. Like Dakota, I longed for lasting, meaningful friendships. The group of men I met at 5:00 AM on Thursdays provided much-needed accountability and support, but I also prayed for a deep, lasting friendship. God answered my prayers by bringing a "ride or die" friend into my life, someone who has been there through every season, just like Dee Rock for Dakota.

Ride or Die: A Friendship to the End

Dakota and Dee Rock's friendship exemplified the kind of relationship everyone needs—a friendship where you can carry each other to the end. Their bond was not just about shared experiences but a shared commitment to each other and God.

They inspired each other to live out Proverbs 27:17: "As iron sharpens iron, so one person sharpens another." Their friendship sharpened their faith, character, and resolve. They knew that no matter what life threw at them, they would stand together like Ruth and Naomi and support each other to the very end.

Through these revolving door relationships, Dakota's faith was strengthened and enriched with lasting friendships. Dee Rock became the embodiment of a "ride or die" friend, someone who would be there through every trial and triumph, carrying each other to the end.

I Can't Carry It For You... But I Can Carry You: An Epic Revolving Door Story

Dakota's journey of faith and friendship had been a revolving door of relationships, each one playing a crucial role in shaping his life. From his early days of seeking accountability and support to forming deep, lasting friendships, Dakota's story intertwined with the themes of loyalty, mentorship, and unwavering support.

A Fellowship of Support

Like Frodo and Sam in "The Lord of the Rings," Dakota experienced the profound impact of having someone who could carry him when the burden became too heavy. Sam's declaration to Frodo, "I can't carry it for you, but I can carry you," epitomized the essence of Dakota's relationships. Whether it was Elan, Chayton, or Dee Rock, each friend stood by Dakota, carrying him through the darkest times when he could not carry the burden alone.

Faith in Action: The Paralyzed Man and His Friends

Dakota's story also mirrored the account in Luke 5:17-20, where a group of friends carried a paralyzed man to Jesus. Their faith and determination to help their friend find healing were echoed in Dakota's life. When Dakota struggled with the weight of his journey, his friends—like the men in the Bible—found ways to bring him to Jesus, whether through prayer, encouragement, or practical support.

Mentorship and Legacy

As Dakota's journey continued, he embraced the mentor role, much like Elijah with Elisha or Paul with Timothy. He poured into the lives of Ashkii and others, ensuring they, too, could carry on the legacy of faith and mentorship. This chain of support and accountability created a ripple effect, where each person Dakota mentored went on to mentor others.

Loyalty and Lifelong Friendships

Ultimately, Dakota longed for a lasting friendship that could stand the test of time. His friendship with Dee Rock embodied this desire—a "ride or die" companionship that echoed the loyalty of Ruth and Naomi. They carried each other through every trial and triumph, demonstrating that true friendship goes beyond mere companionship; it is a bond forged in faith and mutual support.

Conclusion: An Epic Revolving Door Story

Dakota's story is a testament to the power of relationships grounded in faith, loyalty, and support. Like Frodo and Sam, the paralyzed man and his friends, and the many mentors and mentees in his life, Dakota's journey was shaped by those who carried him when he could not carry the burden alone. Whether brief or lifelong, each revolving door relationship contributed to his growth and strengthened his faith.

In the end, Dakota realized that while he couldn't carry the burdens of life alone, he was never meant to. God placed people in his life to carry him, just as he was called to carry others. This epic revolving door story is a reminder that true strength lies not in carrying the burden alone but in the willingness to be carried and to carry others in return.

Through his experiences, Dakota learned the profound truth of Ecclesiastes 4:9-10: "Two are better than one, because they have a good return for their labor: If either of them falls down, one can help the other up. But pity anyone who falls and has no one to help them up." His journey, marked by the unwavering support of friends and mentors, stands as a beacon of hope for anyone seeking to navigate the revolving doors of life with faith, loyalty, and love.

Chapter 6
Panic Doors

Understanding the Panic Door Analogy

Panic Door Analogy for Revelation 3:20 in Chapter 4. We'll explore its significance and how it relates to the broader context of the verse.

In exploring the Panic Door Analogy, we unveil a powerful metaphor within Revelation 3:20. Much like a panic door provides a swift escape in times of urgency, and the verse invites us to consider the immediacy and accessibility of our spiritual connection with Christ. We'll delve into the layers of symbolism, drawing parallels between the physical act of opening a panic door and the spiritual act of inviting Christ into our lives. This analogy becomes a poignant lens through which we examine the invitation extended to us in Revelation 3:20, urging readers to reflect on the urgency and simplicity of a connection with the presence of God.

As Christ stands at the door of the believers heart, the Panic Door Analogy gains depth. We explore the profound insight that, in moments of vulnerability or self-awareness, we may react with a sense of panic, choosing to exit His presence hastily. This emotional response becomes a pivotal theme, prompting readers to question the reasons behind such reactions – fear, guilt, or reluctance. By delving into this dynamic, we unravel the intricate interplay between our human tendencies and the gentle persistence of Christ's invitation. The narrative unfolds, urging individuals to confront their own responses and consider the potential of embracing Christ's presence with open hearts.

The Purpose of a Panic Bar on the Door

Commercial buildings, such as offices, schools, hospitals, and public venues, are required by law to have proper exit devices that provide a safe and secure means of egress in an emergency. One commonly used exit device is a panic bar, a crash bar, or an exit bar.

As a retired assistant fire chief with 20 years of experience. I had to be familiar with the critical role of panic bars in the context of an emergency response. Panic bars, also known as exit devices, are crucial in ensuring occupants' rapid and safe evacuation during emergencies, including fires. Here's a breakdown of their significance in the firefighting context:

Quick and Easy Egress:

Purpose: Panic bars are designed to facilitate swift and easy egress from buildings, especially in high-occupancy areas such as schools, offices, and public venues.

Fire Code Compliance: Building codes and fire safety regulations often mandate the installation of panic bars to ensure compliance with emergency egress requirements.

Preventing Congestion and Delay:

Emergency Situations: During a fire or other emergencies, panic bars prevent congestion at exits by allowing individuals to exit without the need to turn a handle or operate a lock.

Reducing Delay: In high-stress situations, panic bars significantly reduce the time it takes for occupants to exit, minimizing delays that could impede evacuation efforts.

Firefighter Access:

Access for First Responders: Panic bars are designed to allow easy entry for firefighters and other emergency responders from the exterior. This is critical for gaining quick access to the building and initiating firefighting operations.

Securing Re-Entry:

One-Way Exit: Panic bars often function as one-way exits, preventing re-entry from the outside. This feature ensures that individuals evacuate efficiently and emergency responders can access the building unimpeded.

Emergency Exit Signage:

Visibility: Panic bars are often accompanied by clear and visible emergency exit signage. This aids both occupants and firefighters in locating and using the designated emergency exits.

Fire Prevention and Protection:

Life Safety: The primary purpose of panic bars aligns with the overarching goal of life safety during emergencies. Their implementation is vital in minimizing injuries and fatalities by facilitating a rapid and orderly evacuation.

Training and Familiarity:

Firefighter Training: Firefighters are trained to be familiar with various panic bars and exit devices. This familiarity is crucial during emergency response scenarios, allowing firefighters to navigate the building efficiently.

Understanding the function and purpose of panic bars is foundational to effective emergency response, ensuring the safety of both occupants and firefighters during critical situations.

Let's take a look!

Examining the Purpose of a Panic Bar on the door parallels the believer's response to Christ's invitation. Just as commercial buildings install panic bars for swift and safe evacuation during emergencies, believers may sometimes utilize their spiritual panic bars – perhaps driven by life's pressures, doubts, or challenges. Drawing from the legal requirement for safe egress, we draw connections to the spiritual imperative for believers to navigate challenges by entering into a deeper relationship with Christ rather than hastily fleeing. This exploration prompts reflection on the believer's reliance on spiritual panic bars and encourages a reconsideration of their purpose in light of the life-changing presence offered by Christ.

The Story of Debra

In the bustling city of Washington, DC, Debra found herself amidst the daily whirlwind of life. A devoted Christian, she navigated the challenges of a demanding career and the fast-paced rhythm of urban living. Yet, within the sanctuary of her heart, fear and anxiety lingered like shadows.

Debra's spiritual journey became a narrative of her grappling with the demands of faith in a world that often seemed overwhelming. Like the panic bars on the emergency exits of the city buildings, she had developed her own coping mechanisms, a spiritual panic bar, if you will. When faced with moments of vulnerability or doubt, Debra's instinct was to exit the sacred space where Christ awaited hastily.

As she contended with the pressures of her daily life, the symbolic panic bar became her default response. Fear, rooted in the uncertainties of the world around her, prompted Debra to flee from the transformational presence Christ offered. The crowded streets mirrored the chaos within her, and the metaphorical exit door became an escape route from the challenging, sometimes uncomfortable, but ultimately enriching encounters with her faith.

Debra's personal struggle unfolded amid the monuments and corridors of power in the nation's capital. The journey was not about abandoning her beliefs but understanding why she needed to deploy her spiritual panic bar. As she grappled with fear and anxiety, the invitation of Revelation 3:20 echoed in her heart – a reminder that Christ stood patiently at the door, beckoning her to a deeper connection.

The story of Debra became a narrative of redemption, exploring the delicate dance between fear and faith, anxiety and assurance. In the heart of Washington, DC, she discovered that the true strength of her Christian life lay not in fleeing from Christ but in embracing His presence amid the complexities of her worldly existence.

Just as Revelation 3:20 reminded her of Christ standing at the door, Debra found solace in the sacred space she had created within her heart. The challenges she encountered prompted her to reach for her spiritual panic bar – a mechanism honed through life's trials. In those moments of fear and uncertainty, she would hurriedly exit the room where Christ waited, seeking refuge in the familiar escape route she had constructed.

Yet, scattered throughout her journey were whispers from other scriptures. Psalm 34:4 NIV reassured her, "I sought the Lord, and He answered me; He delivered me from all my fears." However, the echoes of Christ's patient knocking in Revelation 3:20 lingered, a gentle reminder that the door she had come to rely on was not an escape from life's tribulations but an entryway into an amazing relationship.

Once she retreated, the door became a silent witness to her internal struggle. Debra wrestled with the tension between the worldly pressures of the city and the spiritual refuge offered by Christ. 2 Timothy 1:7 ESV resonated in her heart, "For God gave us a spirit not of fear but of power and love and self-control," challenging her to confront the root of her anxiety.

One day, as she stood before the symbolic door, Debra felt the weight of Matthew 11:28-30 ESV: "Come to me, all who labor and are heavy laden, and I will give you rest. Take my yoke upon you, and learn from me, for I am gentle and lowly in heart, and you will find rest for your souls for my yoke is easy, and my burden is light.

At that moment, Debra realized that the door she had clung to was not her best friend but a barrier to the profound peace Christ offered. With a deep breath, she turned the handle. She tried to embrace Revelation 3:20 for her life. As the door swung open, she knew that she could find comfort in embracing the presence of Christ, but something kept holding her back.

The door became her best friend.

Debra found solace in the door, a familiar companion in times of adversity. As challenges arose, the door became her refuge, a shield from the complexities of life. She sought comfort in the tranquility of its presence, a retreat from the storm that raged within her.

Yet, unknowingly, the door became an unintended barrier, hindering Debra from fully embracing Christ's transformative presence. Revelation 3:20 echoed in the background, "Behold, I stand at the door and knock. If anyone hears my voice and opens the door, I will come into him and eat with him, and he with me." The invitation lingered, a gentle call that Debra found herself wrestling with.

In moments of distress, the door, once a source of comfort, became a means of escape. Instead of inviting Christ in as a refuge, she turned to the familiar door, closing it behind her, inadvertently shutting out the transformative presence waiting patiently.

The struggle mirrored the sentiment in Psalm 46:1, "God is our refuge and strength, a very present help in trouble." While the door provided immediate solace, it couldn't offer the enduring strength and refuge Christ could bring into her life.."

The narrative urged Debra and those who resonate with her story to consider the unintentional barriers they might construct in seeking refuge. The door, once a trusted friend, now symbolized the choice between temporary comfort and the enduring solace offered by Christ. It was an invitation to open the door not as an escape route but as an entryway for Christ to bring lasting peace and refuge into the depths of her being.

The door became her best friend when things got tough for her. Debra clung to the familiarity of escape in the solitude of her chosen refuge. Yet, Revelation 3:20 echoed like a persistent whisper in her soul, "Behold, I stand at the door and knock. If anyone hears my voice and opens the door, I will come into him and eat with him, and he with me." The invitation lingered, a gentle but insistent call to open the door she had come to rely on.

Panic Doors Manifest in the Churches today.

Panic doors in the church manifest in various ways, reflecting a reluctance or hasty retreat from deep spiritual encounters and challenges. This can be observed through complacency, division, or resistance to engaging with uncomfortable faith aspects. Rather than confronting issues head-on, some may choose to use metaphorical panic doors, hindering the transformative presence of Christ. Recognizing and addressing these manifestations is crucial for fostering a community that embraces Revelation 3:20 – an ongoing invitation to commune with Christ in a profound and transformative way.

As Debra swung open the door to Christ's life-changing presence, she stepped into a new chapter of her spiritual journey. The weight of fear and anxiety began to lift as she embraced the enduring connection that stood patiently at the threshold of her heart. However, she soon realized that she was not alone in this journey.

In the vibrant community of believers in Washington, DC, Debra found companionship and support. Galatians 6:2 ESV resonated in her interactions with fellow believers, "Bear one another's burdens, and so fulfill the law of Christ." As she shared her struggles and triumphs, the once-isolated journey became a collective pilgrimage toward a deeper understanding of faith.

Debra discovered that her story echoed in the hearts of others within the church community. Together, they navigated the challenges of life in the city, finding strength in unity and solidarity. The shared experiences reinforced the truth of Ecclesiastes 4:12 NIV, : though one may be overpowered, two can defend themselves. A cord of three strands is not quickly broken."

As the community embraced Revelation 3:20 collectively, the door of His presence swung open for Debra and many others. The church became where the symbolic panic doors were dismantled, replaced by a shared commitment to face challenges head-on, grounded in the strength of their collective faith.

Simultaneously, Debra observed how panic doors manifested in churches today. The metaphorical exit doors, symbolizing a hasty retreat from deep spiritual encounters, were evident in various forms – complacency, division, or a reluctance to engage with the uncomfortable aspects of faith. The challenge was to recognize these doors and, instead of fleeing, open them to the presence of Christ.

The community embarked on a journey of introspection and renewal, challenging the status quo of spiritual panic doors within the church. Together, they explored how to dismantle these barriers and embrace the fullness of Revelation 3:20 – a continual invitation to commune with Christ profoundly.

Debra's personal journey, now intertwined with the collective narrative of the church, became a testament to the power of shared faith and the dismantling of panic doors. In Washington, DC, amidst the monuments and corridors of power, a community united to face life's complexities with Christ's enduring presence as their guide.

Debra, back to the story

In the vibrant community of believers in Washington, DC, Debra's journey intertwined with the broader narrative of how panic doors manifest in the church. She observed that these manifestations were evident in the congregation's subtle and overt behaviors.

Having opened the door to Christ's presence in her life, Debra became acutely aware of the various ways panic doors could hinder spiritual growth in the church community. Complacency often lurked as a subtle manifestation, with some members content with surface-level engagement, hesitant to delve into the deeper, sometimes uncomfortable, aspects of faith.

In her interactions, Debra noticed moments of division, where differing perspectives led to fractures within the community. These divisions acted as metaphorical panic doors, preventing the unity and strength found in shared faith. The community, however, was not without hope.

Drawing from her own experience, Debra became a voice for dismantling these panic doors. She shared her story, encouraging others to embrace the presence of Christ rather than resorting to hasty retreats. Together, they acknowledged that Revelation 3:20 was not just an individual invitation but a communal one, urging the congregation to open their collective hearts to the enduring companionship of Christ.

The church community embarked on a journey of introspection and renewal. As they addressed complacency, divisions, and the resistance to engage with uncomfortable truths, they began dismantling the metaphorical panic doors. Debra's role became pivotal – her openness inspired others to share their struggles, fostering a culture of vulnerability and authenticity.

Through collective efforts, the church community sought to redefine how Revelation 3:20 operated within their congregation. Once a symbol of retreat, the door became an entryway into shared growth, deepening relationships, and a more profound understanding of their faith.

Debra's journey, now intricately woven into the fabric of the church community, showcased the power of confronting and dismantling panic doors. In the heart of Washington, DC, amidst the complexities of urban life, the church became a beacon of unity and strength, grounded in the enduring presence of Christ and a shared commitment to open doors rather than closing them.

Coping with Panic Doors: Faith, Support, and Counseling

As Debra continued her journey within the church community, she encountered others grappling with their panic doors. Recognizing the need for coping mechanisms, the congregation sought to integrate faith, support, and counseling into their collective approach to address these challenges.

Debra became a beacon of support, embodying Galatians 6:2 as she bore the burdens of those wrestling with their panic doors. The church community embraced the understanding that tackling these spiritual obstacles required a holistic approach. They turned to Psalm 34:18 NLT for guidance, The LORD is close to the brokenhearted; he rescues those whose spirits are crushed.," emphasizing the importance of faith as a foundational pillar in overcoming panic doors.

Support groups within the church became a space for open dialogue and shared vulnerability. Debra's willingness to share her own struggles set the tone for an environment where members could lean on one another. Ecclesiastes 4:9-10 ESV resonated within these circles, "Two are better than one, because they have a good reward for their toil. For if they fall, one will lift up his fellow."

Recognizing that some struggles required professional guidance, the church also introduced counseling services. Proverbs 11:14 ESV became a guiding principle: "Where there is no guidance, a people falls, but in an abundance of counselors there is safety." Trained counselors within the congregation and the community provided a confidential space for individuals to explore the roots of their panic doors and develop coping strategies.

Debra's journey took on a new dimension as she actively supported others through faith encouragement and even accompanied them in seeking professional counseling when needed. Inspired by her example, the church community saw the integration of faith and counseling not as conflicting approaches but as complementary elements in the journey toward spiritual growth.

Together, they realized that coping with panic doors required a multi-faceted strategy. It wasn't just about opening doors and providing the necessary support and guidance. The congregation embraced the idea that faith and counseling could coexist harmoniously, contributing to each member's overall well-being and spiritual resilience.

As Debra continued to navigate her own path and support others, the church became a space where Revelation 3:20 unfolded as an invitation to commune with Christ and as an ongoing journey of healing, growth, and collective support in the face of panic doors.

Creating Safe Spaces for Those Struggling with Anxiety through small groups that do life together.

In response to the pervasive struggles with anxiety and panic doors within the congregation, the church community embraced the concept of creating safe spaces through small groups that would "do life together." This intentional approach aimed to foster a supportive environment where individuals could share their burdens and find strength in communal faith.

Drawing inspiration from Hebrews 10:24-25 NIV, And let us consider how we may spur one another on toward love and good deeds, not giving up meeting together, as some are in the habit of doing, but encouraging one another—and all the more as you see the Day approaching.," the small groups became more than just gatherings; they transformed into sanctuaries where members could openly address their anxiety and confront their panic doors.

Having experienced the power of community firsthand, Debra spearheaded the establishment of these small groups. In alignment with Ecclesiastes 4:12, these gatherings became a cord of three strands, providing a sense of belonging and shared purpose. The small groups were designed to share in each other's joys and collectively navigate the challenges of anxiety and panic doors.

Within these safe spaces, members found resonance with James 5:16 NIV. Therefore, confess your sins to each other and pray for each other so that you may be healed. The prayer of a righteous person is powerful and effective. The small groups became platforms for transparent conversations, confession, and prayer where individuals could admit their struggles without fear of judgment, reinforcing the idea that Revelation 3:20 was not just about Christ standing at the door but also about fellow believers standing together in support.

Scriptures like Proverbs 17:17 NLT were woven into the fabric of these small groups, emphasizing that " A friend is always loyal, and a brother is born to help in time of need.." Through genuine friendships and shared experiences, the small groups cultivated an atmosphere of trust, empathy, and understanding.

Debra's leadership and involvement in these small groups reflected the impact of a genuine community. The church community, once marked by the metaphorical panic doors, now became a network of interconnected lives, fortified by the shared commitment to confront anxiety through faith, support, and communal living.

As these small groups flourished, Revelation 3:20 echoed in the shared prayers and discussions, emphasizing that Christ's presence wasn't confined to an individual's heart alone but permeated the collective space where believers stood together, dismantling panic doors and embracing the journey of faith.

Navigating Anxiety in the Christian Walk"

A dedicated section emerged in the ongoing narrative of Debra's journey and the church community's collective experience: "Navigating Anxiety in the Christian Walk." This segment dives into the intricacies of how anxiety manifests within the Christian context and the spiritual tools employed to navigate its challenges.

The church recognized that anxiety was a prevalent aspect of the Christian walk, impacting individuals in various ways. Drawing from Philippians 4:6-7, which encourages believers to "not be anxious about anything, but in everything by prayer and supplication with thanksgiving let your requests be made known to God," they emphasized the power of prayer as a foundational tool.

Debra, a testament to the role of faith, shared her experiences of navigating anxiety through prayer. Her story resonated with others who found solace in the understanding that casting anxieties upon the Lord, as stated in 1 Peter 5:7 NIV, Cast all your anxiety on him because he cares for you. It was not a sign of weakness but an expression of trust in God's sovereignty.

The church community also regularly reflected on Psalm 46:1 ESV, " God is our refuge and strength, a very present help in trouble. This served as a reminder that, amidst the challenges of anxiety, God was not distant but intimately involved in the Christian walk, providing strength and refuge.

Navigating anxiety within the Christian walk involved a collective commitment to Psalm 34:14 ESV, "Turn away from evil and do good; seek peace and pursue it." The congregation actively sought peace for themselves and each other, cultivating an environment where anxiety could be openly addressed and confronted.

As Debra continued to play a pivotal role in these discussions, her journey became an integral part of the shared narrative on navigating anxiety. The church community discovered that Revelation 3:20 was an invitation to commune with Christ and a source of enduring strength in the face of anxiety.

This section unfolded as a guide for believers, reminding them that anxiety was not an insurmountable obstacle but an opportunity to deepen their reliance on Christ. Through prayer, shared experiences, and a commitment to seek peace, the church community embarked on a collective journey of navigating anxiety in the Christian walk.

Addressed the Stress through Prayer and Therapy.

In this section of this chapter, Debra's story and the broader narrative of the church community, a critical section emerged: "Addressing Stress through Prayer and Therapy." This segment highlighted Debra's realization that while faith played a significant role, aspects of her journey required the expertise of God-ordained outside professional counseling.

Debra's recognition echoed the wisdom found in Proverbs 15:22 ESV, "Without counsel plans fail, but with many advisers, they succeed." Inspired by Debra's honesty, the church community embraced the idea that God had provided resources, including professional counseling, to address the multifaceted nature of stress and anxiety.

1 Thessalonians 5:16-18 NIV became a foundational scripture, encouraging believers to "Rejoice always, pray continually, give thanks in all circumstances; for this is the will of God in Christ Jesus for you." The emphasis on continual prayer remained, but the community acknowledged that seeking professional therapy was also a valid and God-honoring means of addressing stress.

Debra's story unfolded as a testament to the complementary nature of faith and therapy. James 1:5 guided her understanding, " If any of you lacks wisdom, you should ask God, who gives generously to all without finding fault, and it will be given to you. In seeking professional counseling, she recognized the divine wisdom embedded in the therapeutic process.

The church community, too, embraced the idea that God's provision extended beyond the church walls to include trained professionals equipped to address mental and emotional well-being. Romans 12:2 ESV, Do not be conformed to this world, but be transformed by the renewal of your mind, that by testing you may discern what is the will of God, what is good and acceptable and perfect. Urging believers to be transformed by the renewal of their minds, took on a broader perspective as the community acknowledged therapy's role in facilitating this renewal.

Debra's journey became a beacon of hope as the church collectively addressed stress through prayer and therapy. She emphasized that faith alone did not diminish the value of seeking professional counseling but enhanced the holistic approach to well-being.

This final section showcased a community that understood the importance of both spiritual and therapeutic dimensions in addressing stress. The church became a safe space where Revelation 3:20 was not only an invitation to commune with Christ but also an encouragement to utilize the various resources, including therapy, that God had ordained for the well-being of His people.

Summary To Panic Doors

Debra's story and the church community's journey centered around the theme of confronting panic doors and navigating anxiety within the Christian context. Debra, a member of the congregation in Washington, DC, grappled with fear and anxiety, using a metaphorical panic door as a means of escape.

The narrative explored the Panic Door Analogy, drawing parallels between physical panic doors in commercial buildings and the believer's tendency to retreat from Christ in moments of vulnerability. Revelation 3:20 served as a guiding scripture, inviting readers to consider the urgency and accessibility of their spiritual connection with the Divine.

The story unfolded through various stages as Debra confronted her panic doors. She recognized the symbolism of the door in her life, sought support within the church community, and actively participated in dismantling panic doors collectively. The narrative delved into integrating faith, support, and counseling as essential tools in navigating anxiety.

Small groups emerged as safe spaces, embodying the principles of shared faith and mutual support found in scriptures like Ecclesiastes 4:12. The section on "Navigating Anxiety in the Christian Walk" emphasized the power of prayer, communal reflections on scriptures, and a commitment to seeking peace in confronting anxiety.

The final section highlighted Debra's realization that faith alone couldn't address all her needs. The narrative embraced addressing stress through prayer and therapy, recognizing the importance of professional counseling as a God-ordained resource.

In conclusion, Debra's journey and the church community's collective experience illustrated a process of confronting panic doors and navigating anxiety. The story emphasized the complementary nature of faith, support, and therapy, showcasing a community that embraced Revelation 3:20 as an invitation to commune with Christ and as a holistic journey towards well-being, strength, and unity. The narrative painted a vivid picture of a church community that dismantled panic doors, fostering an environment where individuals found solace, strength, and enduring companionship in Christ and each other.

Chapter 7
Panic Room

The Cave of Safety

In a land where fear ruled and the unknown was the enemy, the Croods lived within the confines of a dark, damp cave. For them, safety was found in extreme avoidance, and their survival depended on rejecting anything new or unfamiliar. The entrance to their sanctuary was sealed with a massive rock, symbolizing their commitment to keeping the outside world at bay.

The Croods had learned to exist but failed to live truly. Their lives were a series of monotonous routines, a never-ending cycle of fear-driven decisions. They found solace in the darkness, convincing themselves that the cave was safest. The flickering flames of their feeble torches barely illuminated the boundaries of their shelter, and they clung to the false security it provided.

One day, a series of unexpected events unfolded as the Croods huddled together in their dark abode. A rumbling sound echoed through the cave, and cracks began to form on the walls. Panic gripped the hearts of the Croods as the ground beneath them trembled. The safety they had built their lives upon was crumbling, and the once-sturdy walls of their refuge now threatened to collapse.

Amidst the chaos, a glimmer of light pierced through the cracks, revealing a world beyond their sheltered existence. Eep, the curious daughter of the Crood family, was drawn to the light. She cautiously approached the opening and peered outside. She saw a world filled with wonders, dangers, and endless possibilities.

Eep's newfound curiosity sparked a change within the Crood family. Slowly, they began to question their limited life within the cave. The transpired events forced them to confront the reality that their idea of safety had been a facade. The panic room they had created was not a place to be permanently stayed in; it was meant to be visited, a temporary refuge in times of crisis.

As the Croods ventured out into the unknown, they discovered that there was more to life than cowering in fear. They learned to navigate challenges, face the world's uncertainties, and embrace the beauty of the journey. The panic room had served its purpose, but it was no longer the only source of safety.

In reflecting upon the Croods' story, the concept of the panic room resonated with a deeper truth. It brought to mind the idea of a panic door, a means of escape and refuge in the face of adversity. This idea found its roots in a timeless source of comfort – Psalm 91.

In the secret place, amidst the chaos of life, a panic door leads to refuge and safety. This door is not a permanent residence but a gateway to a place of peace, preparedness, and divine protection. The panic door is none other than the assurance that, regardless of the storms outside, there is a place of solace within reach. Just as the Croods learned to step beyond the confines of their cave, we too can find courage in knowing that the panic room leads to a secret place of unwavering security – a place where we can abide in the shadow of the Almighty.

The story of Cedric, who found safety and refuge in Psalm 91

Psalm 91 NIV

Whoever dwells in the shelter of the Most High will rest in the shadow of the Almighty.

I will say of the LORD, "He is my refuge and my fortress, my God, in whom I trust." Surely, he will save you from the fowler's snare and the deadly pestilence. He will cover you with his feathers, and under his wings, you will find refuge; his faithfulness will be your shield and rampart. You will not fear the terror of night, nor the arrow that flies by day, nor the pestilence that stalks in the darkness, nor the plague that destroys at midday. A thousand may fall at your side, ten thousand at your right hand, but it will not come near you. You will only observe with your eyes and see the punishment of the wicked. If you say, "The LORD is my refuge," and you make the Most High your dwelling,

no harm will overtake you, no disaster will come near your tent. For he will command his angels concerning you to guard you in all your ways; they will lift you up in their hands, so that you will not strike your foot against a stone. You will tread on the lion and the cobra; you will trample the great lion and the serpent. Because he loves me," says the LORD, "I will rescue him; I will protect him, for he acknowledges my name. He will call on me, and I will answer him; I will be with him in trouble, I will deliver him and honor him. With long life I will satisfy him and show him my salvation."

Cedric's journey through life had been tumultuous, shaped by the unforgiving streets of the south side of Chicago. Growing up amidst the challenges of poverty and violence, he faced the constant struggle for survival. As a 55-year-old man, he carried the weight of decades spent navigating the harsh realities of his environment.

Amid the chaos surrounding him, Cedric found solace and refuge in the words of Psalm 91. Those verses became his anchor, a source of comfort in the storm of life. The promise of dwelling in the shelter of the Most High and resting in the shadow of the Almighty resonated deeply with him. In the stillness of prayer, he would say, "The Lord is my refuge and my fortress, my God, in whom I trust."

The challenges that loomed like shadows over Cedric's life were numerous – the secret traps of crime, the deadly plague of poverty, and the constant threats that echoed through the windy city. Yet, with each trial, Cedric clung to the assurance that the Lord would save him. The imagery of being covered with God's feathers and finding refuge under His wings became a vivid picture of divine protection in his mind.

As Cedric walked the city streets, he carried the shield of God's faithfulness, which guarded him from the fear of night terrors and the arrows of danger that flew by day. He faced the darkness of life with unwavering faith, knowing that the Lord would shield him from the pestilence that lurked in the shadows and the plagues that struck at midday.

In the face of adversity, Cedric stood firm, declaring, "The Lord is my refuge; He is my dwelling place." With these words, he embraced the promise that no harm would overtake him and no disaster would come near his tent. The knowledge that the Most High was his sanctuary gave Cedric a resilience that defied the odds.

Through the years, as he witnessed the struggles of those around him, Cedric held onto the hope embedded in Psalm 91. He stood on the word of a thousand fall at his side and ten thousand at his right hand, and God's promise held true – it would not come near him. His eyes witnessed the punishment of the wicked, but he walked unscathed through the storms.

Cedric's life became a testament to the power of faith in the face of adversity. The angels of the Lord guarded him in all his ways, lifting him when the mountains of life threatened to trip him. He understood that his source of safety and protection was anchored in the Lord.

Cedric called on the Lord in moments of distress, and the divine response echoed in his soul. "Because he loves me," said the Lord, "I will rescue him; I will protect him, for he acknowledges my name." Cedric's prayers reached the heavens, and God answered. In trouble, the Lord was with him, delivering and honoring him.

As the years unfolded, Cedric experienced the fulfillment of the final promise – with long life, he was satisfied, and the Lord showed him salvation. The journey through the south side of Chicago had been arduous, but Cedric emerged not just as a survivor but as a living testament to the enduring power of faith and the refuge found in the shadow of the Almighty.

Peace

Even though Cedric took refuge in Psalm 91, When life is going crazy, he knew after I passed through the threshold of the panic door. There are certain things I find, and one thing that was truly lacking was Peace, so he looked to the following scriptures:

- •1 Peter 5:7
- •Philippians 4:6-7
- •Psalms 46:1

As Cedric continued his journey through the challenges of life on the south side of Chicago, he found that even though Psalm 91 provided him with a profound sense of refuge, there was a yearning within him for a specific kind of peace that transcended the external chaos. In moments when life felt overwhelming, he turned to additional scriptures, seeking the peace that could calm the storms within his heart.

Cedric found solace in 1 Peter 5:7, a verse that echoed the sentiment of casting all anxieties on the Lord, for He cares for you. With these words, he learned to release the heavy burdens on his shoulders. In prayer, he cast his worries, fears, and uncertainties onto the Almighty, trusting that God's care was a balm for his troubled soul.

Philippians 4:6-7 became a mantra for Cedric, a reminder to be anxious for nothing but in everything, by prayer and supplication with thanksgiving, to let his requests be made known to God. The promise of peace that surpasses all understanding became a beacon of hope in the midst of turmoil. Cedric discovered that as he surrendered his concerns to the Lord, a peace descended upon him that defied logic and circumstances.

Within the bustling city streets and the trials of everyday life, Cedric clung to Psalms 46:1, which declared, "God is our refuge and strength, a very present help in trouble." This verse resonated deeply with him, offering a sense of assurance that God was not a distant observer but a present help amid trouble. Cedric took refuge in the understanding that, regardless of his challenges, the Lord was with him, providing strength and a sanctuary for his weary soul.

As Cedric embraced these scriptures, he began to experience a profound transformation within himself. The peace he sought wasn't a fleeting emotion but a steadfast presence that anchored him in the midst of life's storms. The panic door became an escape from external turmoil and a gateway to inner tranquility.

In moments of uncertainty, Cedric would meditate on these verses, allowing the truth contained within them to permeate his spirit. He discovered a profound sense of peace that guarded his heart and mind. The storms of life might rage outside the panic door, but within its confines, Cedric found a sanctuary that went beyond physical safety – a sanctuary of peace that enveloped his entire being.

As he continued his journey, Cedric became a beacon of peace in the midst of chaos, a testament to the transformative power of faith and the assurance that, through the panic door, one could find not only refuge from external threats but a profound and lasting peace that anchored the soul.

Direction and Communication

As life's challenges intensified for Cedric, he found himself uncertain, desperately seeking direction and communication from the Most High. During the storm, he turned to the story of David in 1 Samuel 30.

The story of David in 1 Samuel 30 is a significant episode in his life that showcases his leadership, resilience, and reliance on God. In this chapter, David and his men were absent from their base in Ziklag when the Amalekites raided the city, burned it with fire, and took captive the women and everyone else present, including David's two wives.

When David and his men returned to Ziklag, they found the city in ruins and their families taken captive. Distraught and grief-stricken, David's men were so overcome with sorrow that they spoke of stoning him. During this crisis, David, although deeply distressed himself, found strength in the Lord.

1 Samuel 30:6 (NIV) describes David's response: "David was greatly distressed because the men were talking of stoning him; each one was bitter in spirit because of his sons and daughters. But David found strength in the Lord his God."

Rather than succumbing to despair or retaliating against his own men, David turned to God for guidance and strength. In his distress, he sought direction through the ephod, a sacred object worn by the high priest to seek God's will. Having the priest Abiathar with him, David inquired of the Lord through the ephod.

1 Samuel 30:8 (NIV) recounts David's inquiry: "And David inquired of the Lord, 'Shall I pursue this raiding party? Will I overtake them?' 'Pursue them,' he answered. 'You will certainly overtake them and succeed in the rescue.'"

Encouraged by the divine direction he received, David and his men pursued the Amalekites. They engaged in a fierce battle, and with God's guidance, they recovered all that was taken from them and acquired additional spoils.

The story of David in 1 Samuel 30 highlights several important aspects of his character – his ability to find strength in God during moments of crisis, his leadership in seeking divine guidance, and his determination to confront challenges head-on with faith. This episode also underscores the theme of restoration, as David rescued his own family and recovered everything that had been lost.

Cedric's story parallels David's experience in 1 Samuel 30 in several ways. Much like David, Cedric faced adversity and challenges that seemed insurmountable. In times of distress, both sought solace, strength, and guidance from the Lord.

Cedric, like David, experienced a moment in his life where circumstances became overwhelming. The struggles of living in the challenging environment of the south side of Chicago created a sense of despair. Similarly, to David finding Ziklag destroyed and his family taken captive, Cedric faced difficulties that shook the foundations of his life.

In seeking direction, Cedric, inspired by David's use of the ephod, set aside time for prayer and reflection. The ephod, symbolizing a means of communication with the divine, represented Cedric's earnest desire to connect with God amidst the chaos of life. Both individuals used a sacred space to seek guidance and clarity during their darkest hours.

Furthermore, like David's inquiry about pursuing the raiding party, Cedric sought direction to navigate the challenges before him. Through prayer and reflection, he discovered a sense of purpose and a call to face life's difficulties with courage and determination. Just as David received a positive response about pursuing the enemy, Cedric found empowerment to confront the battles of life with renewed vigor.

The notion of returning to battle, present in both stories, symbolizes a resilience to confront challenges rather than succumbing to despair. Inspired by David's determination, Cedric realized that the panic door wasn't just an escape and a gateway to empowerment and resilience. With newfound direction and communication with God, Cedric faced the uncertainties of life with courage and a sense of purpose, much like David going back out to battle to recover what was lost.

Rest & Refreshment

As Cedric continued to navigate the challenges of life, he felt the weight of weariness settling upon him. The battles he faced, both external and internal, took a toll on his spirit. In search of rest and refreshment, Cedric turned to the timeless words of Psalm 23, finding solace in its promises.

He meditated on the comforting words, "The Lord is my shepherd; I shall not want. He makes me lie down in green pastures. He leads me beside still waters. He restores my soul" (Psalm 23:1-3, ESV). In these verses, Cedric discovered a profound truth – the Lord, his Shepherd, provided for his needs and offered a place of rest and restoration for his weary soul.

The image of lying down in green pastures and being led beside still waters resonated with Cedric's longing for tranquility amid the chaos of life. In moments of quiet reflection, he allowed the promises of Psalm 23 to envelop him, finding a sense of peace that surpassed understanding. The Shepherd, in His infinite care, restored Cedric's soul, breathing new life into his tired heart.

Additionally, Cedric sought inspiration from the narrative of Elijah in 1 Kings 19. After a great victory on Mount Carmel, Elijah found himself fleeing for his life from the threats of Queen Jezebel. Exhausted and despondent, Elijah sought refuge in the wilderness. In his solitude, he encountered the Lord, not in the powerful wind, earthquake, or fire, but in a gentle whisper.

Cedric resonated with Elijah's journey. The pressures of life often felt like powerful winds, earthquakes, and fires, and in the midst of it all, he yearned to hear the gentle whisper of God's voice. Cedric sought that quiet communion with the divine in stillness and solitude, longing for a word of encouragement and direction.

In these moments of seeking rest and refreshment, Cedric learned that true strength emerged from overcoming external challenges and finding inner peace and communion with the Shepherd who restores the soul. The panic door became not only an escape from the storms of life but a portal to a sanctuary where his soul could find renewal.

As Cedric continued his journey, he carried the lessons of Psalm 23 and 1 Kings 19. The Shepherd's promise to restore his soul and the recognition that God often speaks in gentle whispers became guiding lights in Cedric's pursuit of rest, refreshment, and a deepened connection with the divine.

Armed for Battle

Refreshed and strengthened by the rest he found in the promises of Psalm 23, Cedric realized that life's battles required spiritual fortitude and the appropriate armor. Turning to Ephesians 6 and 2 Corinthians 10:4, Cedric sought to equip himself with the spiritual weaponry necessary to face the challenges ahead.

Ephesians 6:10-18 ESV became a blueprint for Cedric's battle-ready attire. Finally, be strong in the Lord and the strength of his might. Put on the whole armor of God that you may be able to stand against the schemes of the devil. For we do not wrestle against flesh and blood, but against the rulers, against the authorities, against the cosmic powers over this present darkness, against the spiritual forces of evil in the heavenly places. Therefore, take up the whole armor of God, that you may be able to withstand in the evil day, and having done all, to stand firm. Stand therefore, having fastened on the belt of truth, and shaving put on the breastplate of righteousness, and, as shoes for your feet, having put on the readiness given by the gospel of peace. In all circumstances take up the shield of faith, with which you can extinguish all the flaming darts of the evil one; and take the helmet of salvation, and the sword of the Spirit, which is the word of God, praying at all times in the Spirit, with all prayer and supplication. To that end, keep alert with all perseverance, making supplication for all the saints,

He recognized the importance of putting on the full armor of God – the belt of truth, the breastplate of righteousness, the shoes of the gospel of peace, the shield of faith, the helmet of salvation, and the sword of the Spirit, which is the word of God. Each piece represented a vital aspect of spiritual readiness.

Cedric fastened the belt of truth around his waist, embracing the unwavering truth of God's Word as his foundation. The breastplate of righteousness guarded his heart, reminding him of the righteousness imputed to him through faith. With the shoes of the gospel of peace, Cedric walked confidently, knowing that the peace of God would guide his steps amid chaos.

He lifted the shield of faith, a steadfast defense against the fiery darts of doubt and fear. The helmet of salvation protected his mind, ensuring God's deliverance. Cedric wielded the sword of the Spirit, the Word of God, in his hand, ready to engage in battles with the power of divine truth.

As Cedric embraced the imagery of the spiritual armor, he understood that his battles were not merely physical or emotional but spiritual in nature. The panic door, once a place of escape, now served as the threshold he stepped forth, fully equipped and battle-ready, into the world outside.

Drawing inspiration from 2 Corinthians 10:4, which declares, "For the weapons of our warfare are not of the flesh but have divine power to destroy strongholds," Cedric recognized that his weaponry was not conventional but had divine potency. He prepared to demolish strongholds and take every thought captive to obey Christ.

Armed with the spiritual weapons of truth, righteousness, peace, faith, salvation, and the Word of God, Cedric faced the battles of life with a renewed sense of purpose. The panic door, once an escape, now became a strategic vantage point from which he could engage in the spiritual warfare that surrounded him. Cedric moved forward, knowing that his battles were not his alone but fought with the divine power that equipped him for victory.

Preparedness

Having armed himself with the full armor of God, as outlined in Ephesians 6, Cedric stood fully prepared for the challenges ahead. He understood the wisdom embedded in the phrase "when the day of evil comes." It was not a question of if but a recognition that trials and tribulations were inevitable in the journey of life.

Cedric embraced the mindset of prepping – a spiritual preparedness for the uncertainties of the future. He internalized the truth that, as a follower of Christ, he would face adversity, challenges, and the day of evil. The panic door, once a symbol of escape, now served as a reminder that he was not exempt from the trials of life but rather equipped to face them head-on.

In his moments of solitude and prayer, Cedric fortified his spirit, reinforcing his commitment to the principles of truth, righteousness, peace, faith, salvation, and the Word of God. He cultivated a resilient faith that did not waver in the face of adversity but stood firm, knowing that his spiritual armor was not just for show but a necessity for the battles he would encounter.

Cedric's prepping extended beyond the armor; it became a lifestyle of constant communion with God, a vigilant readiness for the day of evil. He stayed rooted in the Word, allowing it to shape his thoughts, guide his decisions, and fortify his soul. Once an escape route, the panic door now represented a place of strategic readiness, a launching point into the world where challenges awaited.

As Cedric walked the path of prepping, he became a beacon of strength and resilience for those around him. His life reflected the truth that spiritual preparedness was not only wise but essential in the face of life's uncertainties. The day of evil might come, but Cedric faced it not with fear but with the confident assurance that he was equipped with the divine arsenal to withstand and overcome.

In this state of readiness, Cedric found a profound sense of peace. The storms of life might rage, but he stood unshaken within the sanctuary of the spiritual armor. The panic door, now viewed through the lens of preparedness, became a symbol of empowerment and assurance. Cedric stepped into the world, fully aware that when the day of evil came, he was not alone – he was fortified by the power of God's divine armor.

As Cedric continued to walk the path of spiritual preparedness, he found reassurance and strength in the words of Isaiah 59:19. The verse echoed in his mind like a comforting anthem. This promise resonated with the core of his being.

"When the enemy comes in like a flood, the Spirit of the LORD will lift a standard against him."

In moments of challenge and adversity, when the storms of life threatened to overwhelm, Cedric clung to the assurance that the Spirit of the Lord would raise a banner of defense. The imagery of the enemy coming in like a flood recalled the relentless and overwhelming nature of life's trials, but Cedric is prepared. He has found solace in knowing that a divine standard would be lifted against the torrent.

As he faced the battles of the day, whether personal struggles or external challenges, Cedric was aware that the name of the Lord was to be feared from the West to the rising of the sun. The glory of the Lord, shining from every direction, became a beacon of hope, dispelling the darkness that the enemy sought to cast over his life.

With its spiritual significance, the panic door became a tangible representation of this divine standard. As Cedric stepped through it, he embraced the truth that, in times of adversity, the Spirit of the Lord surrounded him like a protective barrier. The promises of Psalm 23, the spiritual armor of Ephesians 6, and the reassurance of Isaiah 59:19 interwove into a tapestry of faith that guided Cedric's every step.

When the enemy came in like a flood – when trials seemed insurmountable, and challenges threatened to sweep him away – Cedric found strength in knowing that the Spirit of the Lord would lift a standard against the onslaught. The panic room has now become a threshold of divine intervention, a gateway through which the Spirit of the Lord positioned a standard of protection and victory.

Cedric, now fortified by the promises of Scripture, faced each day with a resolute spirit. The awareness of the Spirit's standard lifted high brought a sense of courage and peace, allowing him to navigate the floods of life with unwavering faith. In the face of adversity, Cedric stood firm, knowing that the Spirit of the Lord was his shield and defender, lifting a standard against every flood that sought to engulf him.

The Goal

Embracing the truth of Isaiah 59:19 and the spiritual preparedness drawn from Ephesians 6, Cedric understood that the panic room wasn't a permanent residence. It was a sanctuary, a place of refuge where he could recover, regroup, and receive the divine reinforcement needed to re-enter the battlefield of life.

Cedric meditated on realizing that the goal wasn't to linger in the panic room like a bunker, hoping things would return to normal. Instead, it was a tactical retreat, a strategic pause to recover strength, wisdom, and spiritual insight. The panic room, once seen as a place of escape, became a training ground where he honed the skills needed for the ongoing battle.

He recognized the danger of treating his walk with God like a bunker mentality, where avoidance overshadowed engagement. His spiritual armor wasn't meant for passive defense but for active participation in the conflicts of life. Cedric embraced the call to be an actively enlisted soldier, understanding that the battle was one of love and compassion and spreading the message of hope.

Cedric stepped out of the panic room with a renewed sense of purpose, not with trepidation. He was no longer content with merely surviving; he was called to thrive in the world, actively engaged in the battle of love. Once an exit, the panic room became an entrance into the arena where he demonstrated God's love through his actions and words.

His encounters with others became opportunities to extend grace, understanding, and compassion. Cedric wasn't avoiding the world but actively participating in it, conveying hope and redemption. The panic room became a place he visited for rest and restoration, not a dwelling for complacency.

The idea of being a bunker believer faded as Cedric embraced his role as an enlisted soldier in the battle of love. His faith wasn't static; it was dynamic, flowing into every aspect of his life. The panic door served as a reminder that recovery was essential, but so was re-entering the world with a mission to share the transformative power of God's love.

As Cedric moved through the world with intentionality, he understood that waiting for help wasn't about passivity but about relying on the guidance of the Spirit to navigate challenges. His faith wasn't a retreat but a deployment into the frontlines of a world in desperate need of love and grace.

In the battle of love, Cedric found fulfillment and purpose. The panic room, with its divine refuge, was a crucial part of his journey, but the world outside needed the light he carried within. Cedric, now a fully engaged soldier, understood that the call to duty was to actively love and serve others, making a tangible difference in those around him.

Boat as a bunker

Cedric's understanding of the panic room as a refuge rather than a permanent dwelling resonated deeply as he recalled the disciples' experience on the boat in Matthew 14:22-33 NIV.

Immediately Jesus made the disciples get into the boat and go on ahead of him to the other side, while he dismissed the crowd. After he had dismissed them, he went up on a mountainside by himself to pray. Later that night, he was there alone, and the boat was already a considerable distance from land, buffeted by the waves because the wind was against it. Shortly before dawn Jesus went out to them, walking on the lake. When the disciples saw him walking on the lake, they were terrified. "It's a ghost," they said, and cried out in fear. But Jesus immediately said to them: "Take courage! It is I. Don't be afraid." "Lord, if it's you," Peter replied, "tell me to come to you on the water." "Come," he said. Then Peter got down out of the boat, walked on the water and came toward Jesus. But when he saw the wind, he was afraid and, beginning to sink, cried out, "Lord, save me!" Immediately Jesus reached out his hand and caught him. "You of little faith," he said, "why did you doubt?" And when they climbed into the boat, the wind died down. Then those who were in the boat worshiped him, saying, "Truly you are the Son of God."

During a storm, he reflected on how the disciples used the boat as a bunker, a place of perceived safety from the turbulent waters. Yet, Peter dared to leave the boat when he saw Jesus walking on the water. Peter recognized that true refuge was not found in the boat but in the presence of the One who defied the storms.

Cedric saw a parallel in his own life – the panic room was like the disciples' boat, a place to find momentary shelter. But just like Peter, Cedric understood that the true refuge was not in staying within the confines of fear but in stepping out toward Jesus.

When Peter asked if Jesus was truly walking on the water, Jesus didn't immediately calm the storm. Instead, He invited Peter to come to Him during the storm. At that moment, the panic room transformed into a place of dynamic refuge. Cedric realized that, like Peter, he was invited not to escape challenges but to find strength, peace, and purpose in their midst.

Peter stepped out in faith, walking on the water toward Jesus, but when fear crept in, he began to sink. Even in Peter's failure, Jesus extended a hand, caught him, and then placed him back in the boat – the familiar, seemingly safe place.

As Cedric contemplated this scene, he recognized that the panic room, like the boat, was a space where he could find refuge, regroup, and worship the One who could calm the storms. The panic door, the access point to this refuge, symbolized not a retreat from challenges but a deliberate choice to run towards God, finding refuge in His strength and love.

The realization that the panic room was not meant for isolation but for preparation propelled Cedric back into the world with renewed vigor. Even when the presence of God moved mightily in the panic room – just as Jesus walked on the water – Cedric understood that he was meant to carry that presence into the stormy seas of life.

As Cedric walked through the panic room, he embraced the truth that running towards God wasn't an escape from problems but a journey toward the One who could aid and empower. With its carefully planned refuge, the panic room became a launchpad for Cedric to engage with the world, not as a bunker believer but as an actively enlisted soldier in the battle of love, carrying the transformative power of God's presence wherever he went.

As Cedric continued to navigate the challenges of his faith on the south side of Chicago, he discovered profound parallels between his journey and the story of The Croods. The Croods, living in a cave and avoiding anything new, mirrored the tendency of some believers to retreat into a bunker mentality, seeking safety in familiar surroundings and avoiding the unpredictable nature of the world.

The concept of the panic room, inspired by The Croods' cave, took on a dual meaning for Cedric. It became a place of refuge, akin to the cave, but not for the purpose of isolation. Instead, it was a strategic sanctuary where he could find restoration, equip himself for the challenges ahead, and connect with the divine in preparation for his role as an actively enlisted soldier in the battle of love.

Cedric drew inspiration from Psalm 91, learning that the refuge provided by the panic room was not an escape from life's challenges but a fortified space where he could confront them with faith and resilience. The panic room, echoing the disciples' boat, symbolized not an exit from the world but an entrance into a place where divine strength and courage were found.

Conclusion

The story of The Croods illustrated the limitations of extreme avoidance, while Cedric's journey illuminated the potential of a faith that actively engaged with the world. Cedric's understanding of the panic room evolved from a place of mere escape to a dynamic refuge where he found spiritual armor, sought divine direction, and rested in the promises of Scripture.

The concluding chapters of Cedric's story emphasize the importance of not staying in the panic room but going out into the world with a mission of love. He discovered that the church building, much like the panic room, was not a permanent residence but a place to gather, worship, and be equipped for the mission ahead.

In the final analysis, Cedric's journey mirrored the transformative narrative of The Croods. Both stories highlighted the significance of navigating challenges with courage and faith rather than succumbing to fear and avoidance. Having embraced the lessons of the panic room and the battle-ready mindset, Cedric stepped into the world with a heart aflame with love and a spirit fortified by divine strength. The panic room, once a symbol of refuge, became a launching point for Cedric's mission – a mission to engage with the world actively, carry the transformative power of faith, and spread the love of God wherever his journey took him.

Chapter 8

Barriers

Fear of moving forward into your calling

Unraveling Fears

In the sacred text of Matthew 6:34, we find comfort and guidance: "Therefore do not worry about tomorrow, for tomorrow will worry about itself. Each day has enough trouble of its own." This verse serves as a foundational pillar in unraveling the fears that often grip the hearts of those seeking to follow Christ's purposes.

Drawing inspiration from 2 Timothy 1:7, which states, "For God has not given us a spirit of fear, but of power and of love and of a sound mind," we embark on a journey to understand that fear is not divinely ordained. Instead, it is a hindrance that can be overcome through faith, love, and a clear, focused mind.

Psalm 23:4 offers comfort in the face of fear: "Even though I walk through the darkest valley, I will fear no evil, for you are with me; your rod and your staff, they comfort me." This verse encourages us to recognize the constant presence of God, providing strength and comfort as we navigate the challenges of following Christ's purposes.

Philippians 4:6-7 urges believers: "Do not be anxious about anything, but in every situation, by prayer and petition, with thanksgiving, present your requests to God. And the peace of God, which transcends all understanding, will guard your hearts and your minds in Christ Jesus." Through prayer and gratitude, we can actively release our fears, allowing the peace of God to prevail in our hearts.

As we reflect on these verses, let us unravel the fears that entangle our spirits and hinder our journey toward Christ's purposes and calling. By embracing the wisdom and comfort in these scriptures, we pave the way for a fearless pursuit of the amazing path. Now, let us see how these scriptures played a part in Jeff's journey.

In the small town of Nashville, Indiana, Jeff found himself at a crossroads, standing on the brink of a life-changing journey toward Christ's purposes. As he grappled with uncertainties about the future, the words from Matthew 6:34, "Therefore do not worry about tomorrow, for tomorrow will worry about itself. Each day has enough trouble of its own." echoed in his mind, reminding him not to worry about tomorrow. Yeah, that is easier said than done. Jeff began to unravel the fears that entangled his heart, realizing that each day held its own challenges, and God's wisdom encouraged him to face them with faith.

Amidst the shadows of doubt, Jeff discovered the strength within through 2 Timothy 1:7. "For God has not given us a spirit of fear, but of power and of love and of a sound mind," we embark on a journey to understand that fear is not divinely ordained. Instead, as he immersed himself in the scripture, he understood that fear did not originate from the Father; instead, it is a hindrance that can be overcome through faith, love, and a clear, focused mind. With this realization, Jeff confronted his anxieties, recognizing that he possessed the inner strength to overcome any hindrance on his journey.

In the quiet moments of reflection, Jeff sought refuge in Psalm 23. The LORD is my shepherd, I lack nothing. He makes me lie down in green pastures, he leads me beside quiet waters,

he refreshes my soul. He guides me along the right paths for his name's sake. Even though I walk through the darkest valley, I will fear no evil, for you are with me; your rod and your staff, they comfort me. You prepare a table before me in the presence of my enemies. You anoint my head with oil; my cup overflows. Surely your goodness and love will follow me all the days of my life, and I will dwell in the house of the LORD forever. Psalm 23:4 stood out the most and became a beacon of comfort as he navigated the darkest valleys of uncertainty. With the assurance that God was with him, Jeff learned to fear no evil, finding comfort in the Father's presence that guided him through the challenges of following Christ's purposes.

As he continued to search for an anchor to keep him afloat, Jeff tried to latch on to Philippians 4:6-7 "Do not be anxious about anything, but in every situation, by prayer and petition, with thanksgiving, present your requests to God. And the peace of God, which transcends all understanding, will guard your hearts and your minds in Christ Jesus. This became Jeff's anchor as he faced the daunting task of unraveling his fears through prayer and gratitude. In the stillness of his heart, Jeff presented his concerns to God, realizing that surrendering his anxieties opened the door to a peace that surpassed understanding. The peace of God became a fortress, guarding Jeff's heart and mind in Christ Jesus. As fear would start to creep into his mind, he would reflect on Jesus' words in John 14:27 Peace I leave with you; my peace I give you. I do not give to you as the world gives. Do not let your hearts be troubled, and do not be afraid.

Despite Jeff's sincere efforts to absorb the wisdom of the scriptures and internalize their messages, fear continued to cast its shadow, leaving him in a state of procrastination. The town of Nashville witnessed Jeff grappling with the inertia that fear had imposed on his journey toward Christ's purposes.

Jeff found himself revisiting Matthew 6:34 in moments of contemplation, yet the worries about tomorrow lingered. The fear of the unknown still whispered doubts in his ear, hindering the decisive steps needed for progress. Despite understanding that each day carried its own challenges, the weight of uncertainty paralyzed him, making it difficult to take tangible actions.

Though 2 Timothy 1:7 had instilled in Jeff the recognition of his inner strength, the practical application of that strength seemed elusive. The fear of failure and inadequacy created a barrier, causing Jeff to hesitate in the face of opportunities that could propel him forward. The words of power, love, and a sound mind echoed, but the manifestation of these qualities in his actions remained a struggle. I, too, can relate to Jeff in this instance. Knowing the word, quoting the verses while having everything at my disposal to move forward, I waver and feel paralyzed because of my own feelings of inadequacies, which then creates a roadblock, and in return, I get nothing done.

Even the comforting assurance of Psalm 23:4, with its promise of God's presence in the darkest valleys, couldn't fully dispel Jeff's hesitation. The fear of making wrong decisions and walking down uncertain paths left him hesitant, questioning whether he could truly trust the Father's guidance that was offered.

Philippians 4:6-7, an anchor he held onto, felt like the chain had broken. Once, a source of solace seemed distant as the weight of fear led to procrastination. Though genuine, Jeff's prayers were accompanied by a lingering doubt that hindered the full surrender of his anxieties. The peace that surpassed understanding felt just out of reach as fear kept him captive. Procrastination has also been a friend of mine, but it is the enemy of progress. Like Jeff, I always end up in pain when I procrastinate. I will wait until the last minute, which causes anxiety because I find myself rushing, and the end result is not a great product that usually results in pain.

During this struggle, Jeff grappled with external challenges and the internal battle against fear's grip on his actions. Despite embracing the scriptures, the journey toward overcoming procrastination and fully stepping into Christ's purposes appeared to be a process that required Jeff to confront and conquer the persistent fears that held him back.

Jeff struggles.

Jeff's struggles are partly concerned with how others view what God has told him to pursue and what they would say. He also struggles with wondering if he has enough in him for the task given. He needs a constant reminder to lean on the lord and not himself. He knows his validation must come from Galatians 1:10 and not man. Am I now trying to win the approval of human beings or of God? Or am I trying to please people? If I were still trying to please people, I would not be a servant of Christ.

Jeff's internal battle extended beyond his personal fears; the external pressures and opinions of others weighed heavily on his shoulders. The town of Nashville buzzed with speculation about Jeff's chosen path, and the fear of judgment became an additional hurdle in his journey toward Christ's purposes.

Galatians 1:10 became a lifeline for Jeff, a constant reminder that his validation came from the Lord, not the opinions of those around him. As he grappled with the fear of societal judgment, this scripture became another anchor(hoping this chain doesn't pop), grounding him in the understanding that seeking approval from God was paramount.

In moments of self-doubt, Jeff found strength in Philippians 4:13, "I can do all things through Christ who strengthens me." The fear of inadequacy, of not having enough within himself for the tasks set before him, was met with the empowering truth that Christ's strength would sustain him. This scripture became a mantra, reinforcing that his abilities were not confined to his limitations but amplified through divine support.

Jeff's journey took a turn as he embraced 2 Corinthians 12:9, "But he said to me, 'My grace is sufficient for you, for my power is made perfect in weakness.'" This verse became a balm for his insecurities, assuring him that God's grace was enough to fill the gaps in his perceived inadequacies. Jeff learned that leaning on the Lord in moments of weakness was not a sign of defeat or weakness but an acknowledgment of Christ's sufficiency.

The townsfolk's opinions and societal expectations gradually faded into the background as Jeff focused on Colossians 3:23: "Whatever you do, work at it with all your heart, as working for the Lord, not for human masters." This scripture encouraged Jeff to shift his perspective, reminding him that his endeavors were ultimately for the Lord's approval, not the fleeting recognition of others.

As Jeff grappled with his fears, the scriptures served as beacons of guidance, gently nudging him to lean on the Lord and find validation in Christ's approval. The struggle persisted, but armed with these foundational truths; Jeff began to inch closer to breaking free from the shackles of fear and external validation, realizing that the Lord's purpose and affirmation were paramount on his journey.

Jeff found comfort in the company of biblical figures who, too, faced the fear of being used by God. Reflecting on Moses' initial reluctance in Exodus 4:10, "But Moses said to the Lord, 'Oh, my Lord, I am not eloquent, either in the past or since you have spoken to your servant, but I am slow of speech and of tongue,'" Jeff realized that even great leaders grappled with self-doubt when called to a divine purpose.

David, the shepherd turned king, echoed Jeff's sentiments in Psalm 25:1-2, "To you, O Lord, I lift up my soul. O my God, in you I trust; let me not be put to shame; let not my enemies exult over me." These words became a comforting prayer for Jeff as he navigated the fear of failure and the pressure of potential shame from those who doubted his path.

Jeremiah's hesitancy mirrored Jeff's as he questioned his own abilities in Jeremiah 1:6, "Ah, Lord God! Behold, I do not know how to speak, for I am only a youth." This scripture became a shared narrative, a reminder that age and perceived limitations were not obstacles insurmountable by God's guidance.

Joshua's apprehension before leading the Israelites in Joshua 1:9 inspired Jeff: "Have I not commanded you? Be strong and courageous. Do not be frightened, and do not be dismayed, for the Lord your God is with you wherever you go." The reassurance that God's presence accompanied him resonated deeply, encouraging Jeff to press forward despite his fears.

Naomi's journey, as recounted in the book of Ruth, highlighted the theme of loss and transformation. Her resilience in the face of hardship became a beacon for Jeff, teaching him that God could use even the most challenging circumstances to bring about purpose.

Habakkuk's struggle with understanding God's plans gave Jeff a relatable example in Habakkuk 1:2-3. The prophet's questions mirrored Jeff's own uncertainties, reinforcing the idea that wrestling with God's purpose was a part of the journey.

Abraham's initial disbelief when called to father a nation in Genesis 17:17 reflected Jeff's own moments of doubt. The reminder that even the father of faith faced uncertainty fueled Jeff's determination to trust God's promises.

Gideon's reluctance, as seen in Judges 6:15, resonated with Jeff's own hesitation. The notion that God saw potential where Gideon saw inadequacy became a transformative idea for Jeff, encouraging him to view himself through the lens of divine purpose.

As Jeff delved into the stories of these biblical figures, he found comfort in the shared struggles and victories. These individuals' scriptures and lives became companions on his journey, guiding him through the fear of being used by God and reinforcing the transformative power of divine purpose.

Moses: Overcoming Self-Doubt and Speech Impediment

Initially hesitant due to his perceived speech impediment, Moses overcame his barriers through God's reassurance and guidance. Exodus 4:11-12 tells God's response: "Who has made man's mouth? Who makes him mute, or deaf, or seeing, or blind? Is it not I, the Lord? Now therefore go, and I will be with your mouth and teach you what you shall speak." Moses found victory by trusting that God would equip him for the task, conquering his self-doubt.

David: Battling Fear of Failure and Shame

Facing the fear of failure and shame, David triumphed through unwavering trust in God. Psalm 25:2 expresses his reliance on the Lord, seeking protection from shame. David's victories over giants and enemies showcased that trusting in God's strength, even in the face of potential shame, led to triumph and the establishment of his legacy as a renowned king.

Jeremiah: Overcoming Youth and Insecurity

Jeremiah's victory over his fears came through God's affirmation of his capabilities. In Jeremiah 1:7-8, God says, "Do not say, 'I am only a youth'; for to all I send you, you shall go, and whatever I command you, you shall speak." Jeremiah overcame his inadequacy by embracing God's commission, eventually becoming a powerful prophet with an enduring impact.

Joshua: Conquering Fear with Courage

Joshua conquered his fears of leadership through God's repeated encouragement. In Joshua 1:9, God commands him to be strong and courageous. Joshua's victories in leading the Israelites into the Promised Land demonstrated that courage, rooted in God's presence, could overcome the fear of the unknown.

Naomi: Turning Loss into Purpose

Naomi's victory involved transforming loss into purpose. Despite her initial despair, the story of Ruth reveals how God used her hardships to bring about redemption. Naomi overcame the grief barrier by embracing the unexpected ways God could work through her life.

Habakkuk: Understanding God's Plans

Habakkuk's victory lay in gaining a deeper understanding of God's plans. Through dialogue with God in the book of Habakkuk, the prophet moved from questioning to acceptance. He overcame the barrier of uncertainty by trusting in God's wisdom and sovereignty, finding peace amid perplexity.

Abraham: Trusting in God's Promises

Abraham's victory came through unwavering trust in God's promises. Despite initial disbelief in his ability to father a nation, Abraham's faith grew. Romans 4:20-21 highlights his triumph: "No distrust made him waver concerning the promise of God, but he grew strong in his faith." Abraham overcame doubts by relying on God's faithfulness.

Gideon: Recognizing Potential in Weakness

Gideon's victory unfolded as he recognized God's potential in his weakness. Judges 6:14 reveals God's assurance: "Go in this might of yours and save Israel from the hand of Midian; do not I send you?" Gideon conquered his feelings of inadequacy by acknowledging God's strength working through him, leading to a triumphant victory over Midian.

In each case, these biblical figures overcame barriers through trust, obedience, and a profound understanding of God's power working in and through their lives. Their victories inspire the understanding that relying on God's guidance can transform perceived limitations into opportunities for greatness. I can identify with each person on this list. The perceived limitations are just that, perceived. If I look at what holds me back from a different lens, I will have a different outcome.

Jeff's journey was not merely a battle against external obstacles but a profound confrontation with the echoes of his past. Deep-rooted fears, doubts, and insecurities are traced back to a childhood marked by a pervasive sense of not being enough and the ache of unmet acceptance. This is a hard pill and a challenge to swallow. For me to take a deep dive into the past to address my present and future, I must leap backward if I, like Jeff, will move forward.

Jeff revisited moments of feeling overlooked and unheard in the quiet corners of his memories. The seeds of self-doubt took root early, and the yearning for acceptance became a silent companion. As he embraced Christ's calling on his life, the barriers weren't just external; they were internal, woven into the fabric of his identity. I can remember my own story of self-doubt and rejection that started when I was about 3 or 4 years of age. I am the next oldest child of four siblings and the one who desires the most attention. My mother ingrained in me that I was too sensitive and needy. This negatively impacted my life and would carry me to adulthood. Looking for love and acceptance from a woman's embrace had become the story of my life. The reality is I was searching for my mother's acceptance in the arms of these women. Let's get back to Jeff's story.

However, Jeff's story took a turn as he faced these shadows head-on. Recognizing that the call he felt was stronger than the echoes of his past, he embarked on a journey of self-discovery and healing. Through prayer, introspection, and leaning on the scriptures, he gradually dismantled the stronghold of childhood insecurities.

Galatians 1:10, Jeff's mantra, played a pivotal role in this inner transformation. The realization that seeking God's approval mattered more than the echoes of childhood rejection liberated him from the shackles of people-pleasing. Day by day, Jeff learned to stand firm in the assurance that his worth and validation came from the Creator, who designed him for a purpose.

Yet, the journey was not without its challenges. Daily, Jeff confronted the remnants of childhood wounds that surfaced in moments of uncertainty. The fear of not being enough lingered at the edges of his consciousness, threatening to undermine his strides toward Christ's purposes.

Jeff turned to the stories of Moses, David, Jeremiah, Joshua, Naomi, Habakkuk, Abraham, and Gideon in these moments. Their struggles mirrored his own as they do mine, and their victories became beacons of hope. The scriptures, once words on a page, became living narratives of triumph over adversity.

As Jeff stood at the intersection of his past and present, he found strength in the understanding that his identity was no longer defined by childhood wounds but by the grace and purpose bestowed upon him by a loving God. The scars remained, but they were transformed into markers of resilience and growth. He didn't look upon the scars of the past as things to keep him shackled, but they are now viewed from a place of victories that he overcame.

Jeff's journey encapsulated the profound truth that overcoming barriers wasn't merely about conquering external challenges but also facing internal battles that shaped his identity. Through faith, prayer, and a reliance on God's guidance, Jeff emerged victorious, breaking free from the chains of childhood insecurities to embrace the life-changing power of following Christ's purposes.

In the quiet moments of reflection, Jeff stumbled upon Luke 3:21-22, a passage that profoundly confirmed his newfound identity and worth. As he read the words, "Now when all the people were baptized, and when Jesus also had been baptized and was praying, the heavens were opened, and the Holy Spirit descended on him in bodily form, like a dove; and a voice came from heaven, 'You are my beloved Son; with you, I am well pleased.'"

These divine words echoed in Jeff's heart, becoming a personalized message from the Father. "This is my son, whom I love and am well pleased," whispered through the corridors of Jeff's soul, transforming his understanding of self. In those words, he found the ultimate confirmation — a divine embrace that overshadowed the shadows of childhood insecurities.

As Jeff embraced this heavenly proclamation, it became his anthem of victory over the lingering doubts and fears. He carried these words as a shield, a constant reminder that his worth was not defined by past wounds or external judgments but by the unconditional love and pleasure of the Creator.

This confirmation from Luke 3:21-22 became a cornerstone in Jeff's journey, a source of strength when faced with the remnants of old insecurities. He would recall the heavenly declaration in moments of doubt, reaffirming his identity as a beloved son intimately known and cherished by God.

And so, Jeff's story became a testament to the power of divine affirmation. Through the lens of Luke 3:21-22, he discovered a profound truth — that he was not just overcoming barriers; he was stepping into the fullness of the identity spoken over him by a loving Father: "This is my son, whom I love and am well pleased."

Through this amazing journey, Jeff discovered that fear was not an insurmountable barrier but a challenge that could be conquered through faith, love, and unwavering support in the scriptures. As Jeff embraced the wisdom in these verses, his heart became unburdened, paving the way for a fearless pursuit of Christ's purposes.

Navigating Uncertainty

As Jeff's journey unfolded, the uncharted territory of uncertainty emerged as a formidable barrier, casting shadows on his path toward Christ's purposes. The ambiguity inherent in following a profound call on his life brought forth many challenges that tested Jeff's resolve and faith.

Embracing Faith in the Face of Doubt

Uncertainty bore the weight of unanswered questions that lingered in Jeff's mind like unspoken fears. Probing doubts about the practicality of his decisions and the potential outcomes of following Christ's purposes became heavy burdens. The scripture in Hebrews 11:1 emphasizes that faith is the assurance of things hoped for, the conviction of things not seen, and seems like a distant beacon in the fog of uncertainty. Jeff had to lean in on the unwavering belief that, though the road ahead might be unclear, his faith provided a steady foundation. In moments of doubt, he recalled the story of Abraham from Genesis 12:1. God's call to leave his country and go to a land unknown required Abraham to step out in faith. Jeff, too, found inspiration in Abraham's journey, realizing that uncertainty often precedes extraordinary revelations of God's divine purpose. I can remember being faced with a similar challenge to Abraham in 2013.

Being a Federal Firefighter allows us to work in and out of the country in the Department of Defense system DOD. At some point in my career, I always had it in mind to go overseas and work in a different country. Coming from the Bronx, NY, my father always told me to want more out of life than he could provide for me. Never really ventured out of NY growing up other than Virginia, and this seems to be my opportunity. Now, I must say that I joined the Navy at 19 years old and was in for 4 ½ years before they kicked me out for partying too much. I did travel around the world but was usually drunk when doing so. Needless to say, I didn't remember much about the cities and other countries that I visited. Finally, my opportunity came when I applied for a job in Greece on the island of Crete and was offered the job. I prayed and prayed and prayed some more, even throwing out a few fleeces before God to make sure this was his will for my life. I told my parents I got offered the position, and they were unhappy about me wanting to take it. They expressed their dissatisfaction, asking why you would take your family to a different country and leave your family and friends here. Not having my family's support and leaving my two daughters behind, who had their own, I continued to have probing doubts about God's direction. As the leader and visionary for my family, I knew there would be negative consequences if I took this position on my own merit and selflessness. You see, if I make decisions that are not in line with His will, I will infect my family and those I am responsible for. It also affects those around me because I am (Adam).

On the other hand, if this is God's will and timing, he will provide everything we need due to our obedience. My wife and I agreed that this was the Lord's will and journey on a new frontier to Greece. We lived there for four years, six months, and 25 days. I don't recall the seconds, but I will tell you that God did amazing things in my family's lives through our obedience. Echoing the statement above, realizing that uncertainty often precedes extraordinary revelations of God's divine purpose.

Seeking Guidance Through Prayer and Meditation

Jeff's journey through uncertainty involved intentional moments of prayer and meditation. Following the example of Jesus, who withdrew to pray in moments of decision (Luke 6:12), in these days, he went out to the mountain to pray, and all night he continued in prayer to God. Jeff sought guidance in the silence of communion with God. This practice became a compass, aligning his steps with the divine purpose he sought to follow. The uncertainties didn't disappear, but the assurance gained through prayer became a steady anchor.

Meditating on the words of Psalm 119:105, "Your word is a lamp to my feet and a light to my path," Jeff discovered that the scriptures served as a guiding light amid uncertainty. He leaned on the wisdom encapsulated in the Word, allowing it to illuminate his next steps and dispel the shadows of doubt that threatened to engulf him. Gaining encouragement from Joshua 1:8: This Book of the Law shall not depart from your mouth, but you shall meditate on it day and night, so that you may be careful to do according to all that is written in it. For then you will make your way prosperous, and then you will have good success. He knew that if he would continue to renew his mind by a steady diet of pondering on the word of God, it would dispel those doubts, fears, and uncertainties.

Learning from Proverbs 3:5-6

In Proverbs 3:5-6, Jeff discovered timeless wisdom: "Trust in the Lord with all your heart, and do not lean on your own understanding. In all your ways acknowledge him, and he will make straight your paths." This became a guiding principle, reminding Jeff that navigating uncertainty wasn't about having all the answers but about trusting in the wisdom of the One who did. I remember when I truly submitted my life to the Lord and committed to following Him at all costs, and I needed something to hold me down. This became one of my life's scriptures. Trust in the Lord and not myself anymore. After all, I just lead my life to pain and chaos. Lean not on my stinking thing. Acknowledge or concede to Him all my ways (give up so I can go up. He will give me direction for my life.

Community and Mentorship for Support

Recognizing that he didn't need to navigate the uncertainties alone, Jeff sought the companionship of fellow believers. Ecclesiastes 4:9-10 affirmed community strength: "Two are better than one because they have a good return for their labor. For if either of them falls, the one will lift up his companion." Jeff joined a community of like-minded individuals, finding strength in shared faith and collective wisdom.

He also sought mentorship, drawing inspiration from the relationship between Paul and Timothy. In 2 Timothy 2:2, Paul instructed Timothy to entrust what he had learned to faithful individuals who could, in turn, teach others resonated with Jeff. Guided by a mentor, he gleaned insights from one who had walked a similar path, providing invaluable perspectives on navigating uncertainty.

Finding Certainty in Surrender

As Jeff traversed the landscape of uncertainty, he realized that certainty wasn't found in having all the answers but in surrendering to the guidance of the One who did. Proverbs 3:5-6 became a guiding principle: "Trust in the Lord with all your heart and lean not on your own understanding; in all your ways submit to him, and he will make your paths straight." In surrendering to God's plan, Jeff found assurance that the uncertainties of the journey were purposefully orchestrated for his growth and transformation.

Challenging Societal Norms

Jeff's unwavering commitment to follow Christ's purposes stood in stark contrast to the prevailing societal norms, creating a challenging barrier that demanded resilience and a deep reliance on scriptural truths.

The Struggle for Authenticity

Navigating the tumultuous waters of societal expectations, Jeff found solace in the words of Romans 12:2: "Do not conform to the pattern of this world, but be transformed by the renewing of your mind." This scripture became a cornerstone for Jeff, a reminder that authenticity in Christ required a radical shift from conformity to transformation. The struggle for authenticity was not merely an external battle but a constant renewal of the mind, breaking free from the mold cast by societal norms.

Jeff's journey to follow Christ's purposes unfolded against the backdrop of a new societal force—social media. As he grappled with the pressures of conformity, the words of Romans 12:1-2 became a guiding light, providing wisdom in navigating the complex landscape where virtual expectations intertwined with the tangible world.

Verse 1: "I appeal to you, therefore, brothers and sisters, by the mercies of God, to present your bodies as a living sacrifice, holy and acceptable to God, which is your spiritual worship."

Jeff found himself in a world where presenting oneself wasn't confined to physical spaces alone. Social media platforms served as arenas for self-presentation, where the definition of acceptability and holiness seemed entangled with the metrics of likes, shares, and comments.

Amid curated profiles and filtered images, Jeff grappled with the call to present himself as a living sacrifice. The pressure to conform to societal standards on social media echoed louder, demanding a sacrifice of authenticity for the pursuit of online approval.

Verse 2: "Do not be conformed to this world, but be transformed by the renewal of your mind, that by testing you may discern what is the will of God, what is good and acceptable and perfect."

The world of social media, with its trends and influencers, sought to conform Jeff's digital presence to the mold of societal expectations. The battle for authenticity extended to the virtual realm as he navigated the tension between online conformity and the transformative renewal of his mind.

As Jeff scrolled through timelines and feeds, he discerned social media's subtle yet powerful influence on his perception of societal norms. The perfect images, highlight reels, and constant comparison became barriers to embracing God's good, acceptable, and perfect will.

Jeff faced the challenge of filtering through the noise of virtual expectations to discern God's purpose for his life. The renewal of his mind required intentional efforts to prioritize spiritual values over the fleeting validations of social media.

In the age of digital scrutiny, Jeff's story became a testament to the added complexities of challenging societal norms. Social media, while providing unprecedented connectivity, also presented a unique set of challenges in pursuing authenticity. As Jeff continued his journey, Romans 12:1-2 served as an anchor, guiding him through the intricacies of online and offline spaces and encouraging him to present himself as a living sacrifice, holy and acceptable to God, in every facet of his life.

Fear of Judgment and Rejection

As the fear of judgment and rejection loomed, Jeff clung to Psalm 25:1-2: "In you, Lord my God, I put my trust. I trust in you; do not let me be put to shame, nor let my enemies triumph over me." These verses became a heartfelt prayer, a plea for divine protection against the shame that societal judgment could inflict. Jeff learned to anchor himself in the trust that God's approval superseded the opinions of those who sought to undermine his journey.

Balancing Faith Amongst Pressures

Galatians 1:10 became a guiding principle for Jeff as he wrestled with the balance between unwavering faith and societal pressures. "Am I now trying to win the approval of human beings, or of God? Or am I trying to please people? If I were still trying to please people, I would not be a servant of Christ." This scripture was a constant reminder that pursuing God's approval required the courage to resist the gravitational pull of societal expectations.

Finding Courage in Biblical Examples

In addition to the story of Daniel, Jeff drew strength from the experiences of other biblical figures who challenged societal norms. The narrative of Esther, who risked her life to save her people, underscored the importance of courage in the face of societal expectations. Esther 4:14 resonated with Jeff: "And who knows but that you have come to your royal position for such a time as this?" The recognition that his unique journey held a divine purpose emboldened Jeff to face societal pressures with resilience and determination.

The Liberating Power of Authenticity

As Jeff confronted societal norms, he found liberation in Romans 14:12: "So then, each of us will give an account of ourselves to God." This scripture became a catalyst for embracing authenticity as a pathway to liberation. External pressures no longer confined Jeff's journey; rather, they testified to the transformative power of choosing authenticity over conformity. In challenging societal norms, Jeff discovered a profound freedom rooted in the understanding that his ultimate accountability was to God alone.

Trusting God in the Journey

In the complexity of Jeff's journey, trust emerged as a vital thread, weaving through the fabric of uncertainty and adversity. As he navigated the winding paths of life's challenges, the importance of trust in God became increasingly evident, serving as an anchor among the storms and a beacon of hope in the darkness.

Cultivating Trust in God's Plan

For Jeff, cultivating trust in God's plan became a cornerstone of his journey. Despite the twists and turns that veiled the road ahead, he learned to surrender his anxieties and uncertainties to the divine providence that guided his steps. Proverbs 3:5-6 illuminated his path: "Trust in the Lord with all your heart and lean not on your own understanding; in all your ways submit to him, and he will make your paths straight." Jeff embraced these words as a promise, entrusting his journey to the wisdom and sovereignty of God. As he relinquished control and surrendered to God's plan, Jeff found a profound sense of peace amidst life's uncertainties. The barriers that once seemed impossible became opportunities for growth and spiritual transformation. Psalm 56:3 became his mantra: "When I am afraid, I put my trust in you." Jeff learned to lean into his faith, finding solace in the steadfast presence of the Creator, who walked alongside him through every trial and triumph.

Embracing Trust in God's Timing

In addition to trusting in God's plan, Jeff learned to embrace trusting in God's timing. Ecclesiastes 3:11 reminded him, "He has made everything beautiful in its time." Jeff found comfort in the understanding that God's timing was perfect, even when it seemed to diverge from his own expectations. He learned to wait patiently, knowing that each season of waiting was a season of preparation for the fulfillment of God's purposes in his life.

As he surrendered to the rhythm of divine timing, Jeff discovered the transformative power of trust in God's faithfulness. The uncertainties of life became opportunities for faith to blossom, and the trials became steppingstones toward a deeper intimacy with the Creator. Isaiah 40:31 became his anthem: "But they who wait for the Lord shall renew their strength; they shall mount up with wings like eagles; they shall run and not be weary; they shall walk and not faint." Jeff found renewed strength in waiting upon the Lord, trusting His plans were for good, and His promises were true.

Breaking Through

In the multi-facet layer of Jeff's journey, marked by unraveling fears, navigating uncertainty, challenging societal norms, and trusting in God's plan, he found himself at a pivotal moment: the threshold of breaking through barriers that once seemed insurmountable. With faith as his compass and courage as his guide, Jeff stood ready to embrace the transformative potential of overcoming these obstacles.

As Jeff confronted his fears, he drew inspiration from the story of Hannah, a woman who endured years of barrenness and societal ridicule before God blessed her with a son, Samuel (1 Samuel 1). Like Hannah, Jeff learned to pour out his heart before God, trusting His faithfulness and timing even in the face of seemingly insurmountable obstacles.

Challenging societal norms echoed the experiences of the Samaritan woman at the well, who boldly engaged in conversation with Jesus despite cultural barriers and societal expectations (John 4:1-42). Through her encounter with Jesus, the Samaritan woman found liberation and transformation, embracing a newfound identity as a witness to God's grace.

Trusting in God's plan mirrored the journey of Mary, a young virgin who humbly accepted the angel Gabriel's message that she would bear the Son of God (Luke 1:26-38). Despite the uncertainty and potential social stigma, Mary responded with faith and obedience, trusting in God's sovereignty and purpose for her life.

Jeff also found inspiration in the story of Nicodemus, a Pharisee and member of the Jewish ruling council, who approached Jesus seeking spiritual truth (John 3:1-21). Despite his position of authority and societal expectations, Nicodemus humbled himself before Jesus, recognizing Him as a teacher from God. Nicodemus experienced a profound spiritual awakening through their conversation, learning the necessity of being born again through faith in Christ.

Conclusion: Embracing Transformation

Jeff discovered the transformative potential inherent in following Christ's purposes as he broke through the barriers that once held him captive. Through faith, courage, and trust in God, he became a living testimony to the beauty that unfolds when individuals courageously embark on the path laid out by divine guidance.

The journey was not without its challenges, but Jeff experienced a profound sense of liberation and fulfillment in overcoming these obstacles. The unraveling fears, navigating uncertainty, challenging societal norms, and trusting in God's plan were not merely trials to endure but opportunities for growth, resilience, and spiritual transformation.

As Jeff's story unfolded, it became clear that the life-changing power of breaking through barriers extended far beyond his own life. Like ripples in a pond, his courage inspired others to confront their own fears, uncertainties, and societal expectations, emboldening them to step into the fullness of their divine calling.

In the end, Jeff's journey served as a testament to the enduring truth that with God, all things are possible (Matthew 19:26). As individuals courageously embrace the transformative potential of breaking through barriers, they become agents of change, vessels of hope, and catalysts for the realization of God's kingdom here on earth.

Jeff journeyed onward, trusting in God, which emerged as the bedrock of his faith. By cultivating trust in the divine wisdom and timing, he overcame barriers and embraced the transformative power of following Christ's purposes. Romans 8:28 encapsulated the essence of his newfound trust: "And we know that in all things God works for the good of those who love him, who have been called according to his purpose." Jeff's story became a testament to the profound truth that trust, rooted in faith, can turn trials into triumphs and uncertainties into opportunities for divine intervention.

Chapter 9
Closed Doors

The Weight of Expectation

Cory and his sister Cheryl worked the fertile soil of their family's land, their hands calloused from years of labor. As the elder sibling, Cory felt the burden of responsibility on his shoulders. He was to inherit the mantle of his father's toil, expected to tend the earth and bring forth its bounty.

One day, as the sun dipped low on the horizon, Cory and Cheryl approached the altar with offerings for the divine. Cory presented the fruits of his labor, resulting from tireless days spent tending the fields. Meanwhile, Cheryl brought forth the finest of her flock, their wool soft beneath her touch. As the smoke rose from their offerings, Cory watched with bated breath, hoping for approval.

But when the divine favor fell upon Cheryl's sacrifice, Cory felt a pang of jealousy twist within him. His chest tightened as bitterness threatened to consume him. Why should Cheryl receive such a favor? Was his offering not worthy? The seeds of envy took root in Cory's heart, casting a shadow over his joy.

The Battle Within

That night, Cory tossed and turned upon his cot, his mind awash with turmoil. Envy gnawed at his soul, whispering poisonous thoughts into the darkness. Why should Cheryl be favored over you? You are the elder upon whom the burden of responsibility falls. Shouldn't your offering be esteemed above all others?

Cory wrestled with these thoughts, torn between righteousness and resentment. He knew what was right, what his father had taught him. Yet the allure of vindication beckoned, promising consolation to his wounded pride. Why should he suffer the sting of rejection when he could claim what he believed was rightfully his?

The Voice of Reason

As dawn broke, Cory stood again before the altar, his heart heavy with conflict. It was there that the God's voice pierced through the silence, its words a solemn admonition. "Why are you angry, and why has your countenance fallen? If you do well, will you not be accepted? And if you do not do well, sin lies at the door. And its desire is for you, but you should rule over it."

The words struck Cory like a bolt of lightning, their truth resonating within his troubled soul. He knew the path he must tread, the choice he must make. Yet the allure of envy still tugged at him, its grip tightening with each passing moment.

The Consequences of Choice

But Cory's resolve faltered, his pride and envy clouding his judgment. In a moment of weakness, he lured Cheryl into the fields, his heart consumed by jealousy's fire. And there, in the shadow of the crops they had tended together, Cory struck down his own sister, his hands stained with blood and his soul heavy with regret.

As the deed was done, Cory stood amidst the silent fields, the weight of his sin crushing him like a stone. He had closed the door to righteousness, yielding to envy's siren call. And in its wake, only darkness remained.

The story of Cory reverberated through the centuries, a cautionary tale of the perils of envy and the consequences of closed doors. For in man's heart, the battle rages on, a choice between light and darkness, righteousness and sin. And it is in that choice that destinies are forged, and doors are opened or forever closed.

Closing the Doors

As Cory stood amidst the aftermath of his grievous deed, a profound realization washed over him like a chilling breeze. Just as one locks down their house to secure it against intruders, so must they guard the doorways of their hearts and minds against the insidious whispers of sin.

With trembling hands, Cory reflected on the words he had heard at the altar, the Spirit's warning echoing in his ears. "Sin desires to have you, but you must master it." The weight of personal responsibility bore down upon him, a sobering reminder that he alone held the key to his own destiny and the choice was his to make.

Cory made a solemn vow to himself and God in the stillness of the field. He would not allow envy and bitterness to infiltrate his soul again. He would guard the doorways of his heart with unwavering vigilance, ensuring that sin found no foothold within.

With each passing day, Cory worked to rebuild what had been shattered by his own hand. He sought forgiveness and redemption, knowing that true healing could only come from within. And though the scars of his past actions remained, Cory found peace in the knowledge that he had chosen the path of righteousness.

The story of Cory served as a poignant reminder to all who heard it, a testament to the power of personal responsibility and the importance of guarding the doorways of one's own soul. Ultimately, not the darkness defines us, but the light we choose to let in.

Embracing Responsibility

As Cory recalled God's warning reverberating in his mind, he felt a surge of determination coursing through his veins. He knew that he must acknowledge the gravity of his past actions and take full responsibility and accountability for them.

With a heavy heart, Cory sought out those whom he had wronged, offering sincere apologies, and seeking to make amends wherever possible. He was learning to face the consequences of his actions with humility, understanding that true growth could only come from facing the truth head-on.

However, not only his past actions weighed heavily upon Cory's conscience. He realized that he must also take responsibility for his future actions, ensuring he did not succumb to the temptations that had led him astray. Knowing that this will be a tall task during this life journey.

With each new day, Cory resolved to walk the path of righteousness, guided by the principles of integrity and moral fortitude. He understood that mastering sin was not a one-time feat but an ongoing journey, requiring constant vigilance, self-discipline, and internal work within.

As Cory embraced his newfound sense of responsibility, he found strength in knowing that he held the power to shape his future. He vowed to rule over sin, not allowing it to dictate the course of his life any longer.

And so, with a renewed sense of purpose, Cory embarked on a journey of self-discovery and redemption, determined to leave behind the shadows of his past and embrace the light of a brighter future. Cory realized it was never too late to stand up and be accountable and responsible for his actions. When he acknowledges his mistakes and seeks forgiveness, it forges a new path for him that is guided by truth and integrity.

The Narrow Path

As Cory continued his journey of self-discovery and redemption, he reflected on the words of the divine warning: "Sin is crouching at your door; it desires to have you, but you must rule over it." With each step forward, he understood the significance of those words more deeply.

He realized that sin was not always an obvious adversary but often lurked in the shadows, waiting for a chance to seize upon the slightest opening. It was not an enemy that burst through wide-open doors but slithered through the cracks of narrow ones, insidiously infiltrating the heart and mind.

Cory understood that mastering sin required more than just resisting its overt temptations. It demanded a vigilant awareness of the subtle influences that sought to lead him astray. He learned to recognize the deceptive whispers of envy and bitterness, guarding against their insidious advances with unwavering resolve.

But as Cory walked the narrow path of righteousness, he also encountered moments of doubt and uncertainty. The journey was fraught with challenges, and the way forward often seemed obscured by the shadows of his past mistakes.

Yet, in those moments of doubt, Cory found strength in knowing he was not alone. He drew inspiration from the forefathers who had walked this path before him and from the divine guidance of the Holy Spirit that illuminates his way.

With each passing day, Cory embraced the narrow path with renewed determination, knowing that it was not an easy road but one that led to true freedom and fulfillment. He understood that while the wide path may offer temporary pleasures, it ultimately led to destruction. But the narrow path, though difficult to traverse, led to life and peace.

The words of Matthew 7:13-14 echoed in his mind like a guiding light: "Enter through the narrow gate. For wide is the gate, and broad is the road that leads to destruction, and many enter through it. But small is the gate and narrow the road that leads to life, and only a few find it."

Cory pondered these words deeply, understanding the profound truth they held. He realized that the path he had chosen, the narrow path of righteousness, was not easy. It required discipline, perseverance, and a steadfast commitment to truth.

In contrast, the wide gate and broad road symbolized the allure of worldly pleasures and instant gratification. It was a path strewn with temptations and distractions, leading many astray into the darkness of destruction.

But Cory knew that true life, abundant and everlasting, could only be found by entering through the narrow gate and walking the narrow road. It was a path less traveled, requiring sacrifice and self-denial, but it ultimately led to fulfillment and peace.

As Cory continued navigating the narrow path's twists and turns, he encountered challenges and obstacles along the way. Yet, he found strength in the knowledge that he was not alone. The divine presence guided his steps, illuminating the way and providing comfort in times of trial.

Cory's journey involves navigating through the closed doors of temptation and sin while actively seeking out and entering through the narrow doors of righteousness and salvation. By adhering to the teachings of Scripture and staying true to his convictions, Cory learns to discern between the wide and narrow paths, ultimately wanting to choose the one that leads to life and peace.

The Watchful Guardian

As Cory continued along the narrow path, he likened his journey to that of a watchful guardian keeping a vigilant eye on a beloved pet. Just as a responsible owner ensures that their dog stays safely within the confines of their home, Cory understood the importance of guarding the doorways of his heart against the subtle intrusions of sin, like a crack in the door that could easily lead to mischief.

Cory recalled the image of a dog eagerly waiting by the door, its nose pressed against the crack, yearning for the freedom that lay beyond. In much the same way, sin lurked just outside the door of his heart, its enticing whispers beckoning him to stray from the path of righteousness.

With each passing day, Cory became more attuned to the subtle movements of sin, recognizing its stealthy advances and guarding against its insidious influence. Like a vigilant guardian, he remained ever watchful, ensuring that the crack in the door of his heart remained firmly closed against the encroachment of temptation.

The Lord began to speak to Cory through the leans of 1 Peter 5:8 NIV, which states to be alert and of a sober mind. Your enemy, the devil, prowls around like a roaring lion, looking for someone to devour. Cory began to understand the relevance of these biblical narratives. He recognizes that sin is not merely a personal failing but a spiritual battle against the forces of darkness.

Cory sees sin as a prowling predator, ready to pounce and devour anyone who lets down their guard. He understands the importance of being alert and of a sober mind, as Peter advises, and recognizes that spiritual vigilance is essential for guarding against the schemes of the enemy.

By reflecting on this biblical story and heeding Peter's warning, Cory commits himself to remaining vigilant and steadfast in his faith. He resolves to cultivate a spirit of discernment, recognizing the subtle tactics of the enemy and guarding against the allure of sin. Cory understands that by staying grounded in God's Word, prayer, and fellowship with other believers, he can resist the enemy's attacks and open the doors of his heart to God's blessings and favor.

Yet, even as he stood guard against the wiles of sin, Cory found comfort in the knowledge that he was not alone in his struggle. God's presence, like a steadfast companion, stood beside him, offering guidance and strength in times of need.

And so, with his eyes fixed on the narrow path ahead and his heart fortified against the temptations that lay in wait, Cory pressed onward with renewed determination, for he knew that in guarding the doorways of his heart, he could navigate the twists and turns of life's journey with confidence and grace, guided by the unwavering light of righteousness.

Genesis 4:8-16 (NIV)

Now Cain said to his brother Abel, "Let's go out to the field." While they were in the field, Cain attacked his brother Abel and killed him. Then the Lord said to Cain, "Where is your brother Abel?" "I don't know," he replied. "Am I my brother's keeper?" The Lord said, "What have you done? Listen! Your brother's blood cries out to me from the ground. Now you are under a curse and driven from the ground, which opened its mouth to receive your brother's blood from your hand. When you work the ground, it will no longer yield its crops for you. You will be a restless wanderer on the earth." Cain said to the Lord, "My punishment is more than I can bear. Today you are driving me from the land, and I will be hidden from your presence; I will be a restless wanderer on the earth, and whoever finds me will kill me." But the Lord said to him, "Not so anyone who kills Cain will suffer vengeance seven times over." Then the Lord put a mark on Cain so that no one who found him would kill him. So Cain went out from the Lord's presence and lived in the land of Nod, east of Eden.

Cory sees parallels between his struggles and those of Cain. Like Cain, he grapples with jealousy and resentment, feeling the weight of unmet expectations and the desire for recognition and favor. However, Cory recognizes the importance of guarding against the destructive impulses that lurk at the door of his heart, knowing that yielding to such temptations could lead him down a path of ruin, much like Cain's descent into darkness.

Moreover, Cory understands the significance of personal responsibility and accountability, exemplified by Cain's response to God's inquiry about Abel's whereabouts. When confronted with his sin, Cain tries to evade responsibility, asking, "Am I my brother's keeper?" However, God holds Cain accountable for his actions, declaring a curse upon him and banishing him from the land.

In Cory's journey, he learns from Cain's mistakes, realizing he cannot shirk responsibility for his own choices. He understands that the consequences of sin are far-reaching and that they affect him personally and those around him. Through Cain's story, Cory sees the importance of owning up to his actions and seeking redemption and forgiveness.

Cory understands that the choices we make at the door of our hearts have profound implications for our lives and the lives of others. By heeding the warning from Cain's narrative, Cory strives to keep the doors of his heart guarded against sin, choosing the narrow path of righteousness and accountability and thus forging a different fate from that of Cain.

Disobedience and its consequences

As Cory's journey unfolds, he finds himself at a crossroads, grappling with the weight of his decisions and the consequences ripple through his life. His reflections on the stories of Cain and Abel from Genesis 4:8-16 and Saul's disobedience in 1 Samuel 13:2-14 resonate deeply within him, serving as cautionary tales of the dangers of straying from God's path. Here, we pick up on the scripture text of 1Samuael 13:2-14.

1 Samuel 13:2-14 NIV

Saul chose three thousand men from Israel; two thousand were with him at Mikmash and in the hill country of Bethel, and a thousand were with Jonathan at Gibeah in Benjamin. The rest of the men he sent back to their homes. Jonathan attacked the Philistine outpost at Geba, and the Philistines heard about it. Then Saul had the trumpet blown throughout the land and said, "Let the Hebrews hear!" So all Israel heard the news: "Saul has attacked the Philistine outpost, and now Israel has become obnoxious to the Philistines." And the people were summoned to join Saul at Gilgal. The Philistines assembled to fight Israel, with three thousand[a] chariots, six thousand charioteers, and soldiers as numerous as the sand on the seashore. They went up and camped at Mikmash, east of Beth Aven. When the Israelites saw that their situation was critical and that their army was hard pressed, they hid in caves and thickets, among the rocks, and in pits and cisterns. Some Hebrews even crossed the Jordan to the land of Gad and Gilead. Saul remained at Gilgal, and all the troops with him were quaking with fear. He waited seven days, the time set by Samuel; but Samuel did not come to Gilgal, and Saul's men began to scatter. So he said, "Bring me the burnt offering and the fellowship offerings." And Saul offered up the burnt offering. Just as he finished making the offering, Samuel arrived, and Saul went out to greet him. "What have you done?" asked Samuel.

Saul replied, "When I saw that the men were scattering, and that you did not come at the set time, and that the Philistines were assembling at Mikmash, I thought, 'Now the Philistines will come down against me at Gilgal, and I have not sought the Lord's favor.' So I felt compelled to offer the burnt offering." "You have done a foolish thing," Samuel said. "You have not kept the command the Lord your God gave you; if you had, he would have established your kingdom over Israel for all time. 14 But now your kingdom will not endure; the Lord has sought out a man after his own heart and appointed him ruler of his people, because you have not kept the Lord's command."

The story of Saul's disobedience and its consequences in 1 Samuel 13:2-14 serves as another powerful illustration of the importance of obedience and the consequences of acting outside of God's will.

In the context of Cory's journey, Saul's actions highlight the dangers of taking matters into one's own hands and failing to trust God's timing and guidance. Like Saul, Cory may face situations where he feels pressured to act impulsively or out of fear rather than waiting patiently for God's direction.

Cory understands the significance of obedience and the consequences of disobedience, as exemplified by Saul's experience. When Saul grew impatient waiting for Samuel and saw his army scattering in fear, he took matters into his own hands and offered the burnt offering, a task reserved for the priest. Despite Saul's intentions, his actions were ultimately driven by fear and a lack of trust in God's plan.

Similarly, Cory realizes that true obedience requires faith and trust in God's sovereignty, even when faced with challenging circumstances. He understands that acting impulsively or outside of God's will can have far-reaching consequences, just as Saul's disobedience led to the loss of his kingdom.

Through Saul's story, Cory learns the importance of seeking God's favor and following His commands, even when it may seem difficult or uncertain. He recognizes that obedience is not just about following rules but about aligning oneself with God's purposes and trusting in His faithfulness.

Ultimately, Cory's journey is shaped by his commitment to obedience and desire to walk in God's ways. By learning from Saul's mistakes, Cory strives to cultivate a heart that is fully surrendered to God, trusting in His guidance and relying on His strength to navigate the challenges of life's journey.

Samuel's response to Saul's choice serves as a poignant reminder of the consequences of disobedience and the closing of doors resulting from acting outside God's will.

When Samuel confronts Saul about his actions, he rebukes him sharply, saying, "You have done a foolish thing. You have not kept the command the Lord your God gave you" (1 Samuel 13:13). Samuel emphasizes that Saul's decision to offer the burnt offering himself, instead of waiting for Samuel as instructed, was a direct violation of God's command.

Samuel's words highlight the severity of Saul's disobedience and the gravity of his folly. By taking matters into his own hands and offering the sacrifice without authorization, Saul closed the door to God's favor and blessing upon his reign as king. Instead of trusting in God's timing and seeking His guidance, Saul acted out of fear and impatience, leading to the forfeiture of his kingdom.

Furthermore, Samuel's response underscores the principle that obedience to God's commands is paramount for receiving His blessings and establishing His kingdom. Saul's disobedience not only resulted in the loss of his kingdom but also closed the door to God's plan for him to rule over Israel for all time (1 Samuel 13:13).

In Cory's journey, Samuel's rebuke serves as a sobering reminder of the importance of obedience and the consequences of acting outside of God's will. Cory understands that by disobeying God's commands, he risks closing the doors to God's blessings and favor in his life. He recognizes the need to align his actions with God's will and to trust in His timing, even when faced with challenges or uncertainties.

Through Saul's example, Cory learns that obedience is the key to unlocking God's blessings and fulfilling His purposes. By heeding Samuel's admonition and striving to walk in obedience to God's commands, Cory seeks to keep the doors of blessing and favor open in his own life, trusting God's faithfulness to guide him along the narrow path of righteousness.

Just as Cain's jealousy led to fratricide and Saul's impatience, which resulted in the loss of his kingdom, Cory realizes the profound impact of his own choices on his spiritual journey. The closed doors of missed opportunities and severed relationships loom large before him, a stark reminder of the consequences of disobedience and sin.

Yet, amid the darkness of his reflections, Cory finds a glimmer of hope. He understands that the same God who closed the doors of judgment on Cain and Saul also offers the keys to redemption and restoration. Through humility, repentance, and a renewed commitment to obedience, Cory sees a path forward—a path illuminated by the grace and mercy of a loving God.

As Cory stands at the threshold of his own story, he knows the journey ahead will not be easy. But armed with the wisdom gleaned from the narratives of Cain, Abel, Saul, and countless others, he steps forward with courage and determination, for he knows that even the closed doors of the past can serve as stepping stones to a brighter future, guided by the unfailing light of God's love.

Chapter 10:

Fire Doors

You Shall Not Pass

Fire Door:

Meaning: A fire door is a door with a fire-resistance rating used as part of a passive fire protection system to reduce the spread of fire and smoke between compartments. It is typically made of materials that can withstand high temperatures and prevent the passage of smoke and fire for a certain period.

- Purpose: The primary purpose of a fire door is to contain fires in the area where they originated, allowing occupants to safely evacuate and limiting the fire's spread within the building.

Fire Wall:

- Meaning: A firewall is a fire-resistant barrier designed to prevent fire spread between or through buildings. It is typically a wall that extends continuously from the foundation to the roof and is constructed to withstand fire for a specified duration, usually measured in hours.
- Purpose: Firewalls are intended to compartmentalize buildings into sections separated by these walls. In the event of a fire, the wall helps to contain the fire within one section, providing additional time for evacuation and reducing the risk of the fire spreading to other parts of the building.

Fire Barrier:

- Meaning: A fire barrier is a fire-resistant wall, floor, or ceiling assembly that is designed to restrict the spread of fire and smoke within a building. It includes both vertical and horizontal assemblies and has a fire-resistance rating that can vary depending on the application.
- Purpose: The purpose of fire barriers is to create compartments within a building to contain fires, limit the spread of smoke, and protect escape routes, ensuring that

occupants have a clear path to safety. Fire barriers also help protect structural elements of the building from fire damage.

Together, these elements form a comprehensive passive fire protection system that enhances the overall safety of a building by slowing the spread of fire, providing safe evacuation routes, and protecting critical structural components.

Let us now look at the story from the Lord of the Rings.

In "The Lord of the Rings: The Fellowship of the Ring," Gandalf stands on the Bridge of Khazad-dûm in the Mines of Moria. Stating "You Shall Not Pass"

Context and Events:

The Fellowship in Moria: The Fellowship of the Ring, consisting of Frodo, Sam, Merry, Pippin, Aragorn, Gandalf, Legolas, Gimli, and Boromir, are journeying through the Mines of Moria. They are trying to avoid detection by Sauron's forces and to find a safer passage through the mountains.

As they traverse the mines, they awaken an ancient evil— Durin's Bane, a Balrog of Morgoth. The Balrog is a powerful, demonic being of fire and shadow. Orcs and the Balrog pursue the Fellowship. They flee towards the Bridge of Khazad-dûm, a narrow stone bridge spanning a deep chasm. The bridge is the only way to escape.

Gandalf's Stand:

At the bridge, Gandalf realizes that the Balrog poses an immense threat to the entire Fellowship. He decides to make a stand to allow the others to escape. He intends to stop the Balrog from crossing the bridge and pursuing them further.

Protection of the Fellowship:

Gandalf understands that if the Balrog crosses the bridge, it will likely kill or capture the entire Fellowship, dooming their quest to destroy the One Ring. Gandalf's mission is to aid and protect the members of the Fellowship, especially Frodo, who carries the One Ring. Gandalf ensures that the quest can continue by stopping the Balrog, even at great personal risk.

Self-Sacrifice:

As a Maia (a being of great power), Gandalf recognizes his responsibility to confront such a powerful enemy. His stand is an act of courage and self-sacrifice for the greater good.

Gandalf confronts the Balrog on the bridge with his famous line: "You cannot pass! I am a servant of the Secret Fire, wielder of the flame of Anor. You cannot pass. The dark fire will not avail you, the flame of Udûn. Go back to the shadow! You cannot pass!"

Breaking the Bridge: Gandalf strikes the bridge with his staff, causing it to crack and break under the Balrog's feet. The Balrog falls into the chasm, but as it falls, it lashes out with its whip, ensnaring Gandalf and pulling him down into the abyss.

This act of bravery by Gandalf delays the Balrog long enough for the rest of the Fellowship to escape, though it appears to cost Gandalf his life. This pivotal moment underscores Gandalf's role as a protector and his willingness to sacrifice himself for the success of their mission.

Fire Doors – "You Shall Not Pass"

In Brazil's vibrant and mystical land, rich with culture and history, lived a family bound by a dark legacy. This lineage, known as the Menendez, bore a curse that spanned generations, a blight that shadowed their lives and brought suffering to their descendants. The origins of this curse were as old as the family's name, rooted in the transgressions of an ancestor who sought forbidden power.

1. Who: The Bearers of the Curse

The generational curse in Brazil, much like those mentioned in the Bible, affected the descendants of those who had committed grave sins. In the case of the Menendez family, the curse resulted from a pact made by their forefather, Carlos, with a dark entity in exchange for power and wealth. This curse manifested in various forms: misfortune, untimely deaths, and a pervasive sense of despair. Each generation felt its oppressive weight, from Carlos's children to their grandchildren and beyond. The curse's reach extended to all descendants, illustrating the biblical principle found in Exodus 20:5, where the iniquities of the fathers impact their children unto the third and fourth generation.

2. What: The Nature of the Curse

According to biblical understanding, a generational curse is a spiritual consequence passed down from one generation to another due to the ancestors' sins. This concept is vividly demonstrated in the plight of the Menendez family. The curse Carlos invoked was not merely a series of unfortunate events but a binding spiritual chain that brought tangible suffering to his descendants. The family's crops failed, their livestock perished, and inexplicable fires plagued their homes. This idea parallels the biblical passages where generational curses are discussed, such as in Deuteronomy 5:9 and Numbers 14:18, highlighting sin's tangible, often devastating consequences.

3. Where: The Scriptural Basis

The concept of generational curses is found in various books of the Bible, both in the Old and New Testaments. In Brazil, the curse's scriptural counterparts were often recited by the village elders, who drew upon scriptures such as Exodus 20:5, where God warns against idolatry, and Numbers 14:18, which speaks of visiting the iniquity of the fathers on the children. These passages were a grim reminder of the curse's origins and justification. The elders also referenced Ezekiel 18, which provided a contrasting view, emphasizing individual responsibility for sin and hinting at a possible redemption.

4. When: The Timing of the Curse

The generational curse upon the Menendez family was believed to have been invoked during Carlos's time, around the age when he sought power from dark forces. This coincided with the era of Brazil's greatest turmoil, paralleling the historical period of the Mosaic Law in the Bible when such curses were first described. Over centuries, as the curse manifested through various misfortunes, each generation bore its mark, reflecting the biblical timeline that spans from the giving of the Law to Moses to the prophetic writings, emphasizing the ongoing relevance of these spiritual consequences.

5. Why: The Rationale Behind the Curse

The rationale behind the generational curse of the Menendez family, much like in the biblical context, was deeply rooted in the understanding of divine justice and the consequences of sin. Carlos's pact represented a grave transgression against the natural and divine order, warranting severe consequences. This reflected several biblical reasons for generational curses:

Divine Justice: The curse illustrated the holiness and justice of the divine order, which could not tolerate Carlos's sin and its corrupting influence.

Oral Consequences: The tangible misfortunes that befell the Menendez family emphasized that sin has real, far-reaching consequences. This is akin to the biblical narratives where Abraham and Isaac committed similar sins, resulting in consequences that affected not just themselves but their entire households. In Genesis 12:10-20 and Genesis 20:1-18,

Abraham deceived others about his wife Sarah's identity, leading to tension and divine intervention. Similarly, Isaac repeated this sin in Genesis 26:1-11, showing how behavior patterns and consequences can pass through generations, compounding the family's challenges.

Covenant Relationship: The curse underscored the seriousness of the family's covenant with the divine and the need for faithfulness, mirroring Israel's covenant relationship with God.

Human Responsibility: As in Ezekiel 18, the possibility of breaking the curse highlighted evolving understanding and individual responsibility.

The Journey to Break the Curse

Elara Menendez, a young woman with fiery determination and a heart of gold, grew up hearing whispers of the curse but never fully understood its weight until her 21st birthday. In a dusty attic, she discovered an old tome that revealed the dark pact made by Carlos. Determined to end the cycle, Elara set out on a perilous journey through the Brazilian rainforest and the Acaraí Mountains, gathering a group of allies: João, a skilled swordsman; Larissa, a mage; and Tiago, an expert in ancient artifacts.

As Elara delved deeper into her family's history, she came across old, ancient documents chronicling stories of molestation, incest, alcoholism, drug addiction, and all types of debauchery that had been hidden but were manifesting in those who came after Carlos made his pact with darkness. As she read these documents, she realized the true origins of her and her family's dysfunctional behaviors. She saw no sign of healthy relationships in her life or her family's lives. She was reminded of the scripture in Galatians 5:19-21 ESV, "Now the works of the flesh are evident: sexual immorality, impurity, sensuality, idolatry, sorcery, enmity, strife, jealousy, fits of anger, rivalries, dissensions, divisions, envy, drunkenness, orgies, and things like these. I warn you, as I warned you before, that those who do such things will not inherit the kingdom of God." Romans 13:13 ESV, "Let us walk properly as in the daytime, not in orgies and drunkenness, not in sexual immorality and sensuality, not in quarreling and jealousy."

As she contemplated the complexity of her family's pain, she could see that generations of hurt and pain had been passed down through the bloodstream of her family. From great-great-grandparents down to parents, uncles, aunts, cousins, and siblings, a pandemic of pain and hurt had been nesting in the family for generations, and it had to be stopped. Realizing that all these dynamics were in her DNA, she was determined to break the cycle of the past.

Their journey led them deep into the Brazilian rainforest and up the Acaraí Mountains, where the Guardian of the Abyss resided. This malevolent being, much like the dark spiritual forces in biblical narratives, embodied the curse's power. As they traversed the perilous terrain, they were pursued by dark minions of the Guardian, echoing the Fellowship's harrowing journey through the Mines of Moria in "The Lord of the Rings: The Fellowship of the Ring." As Gandalf had done, Elara understood that if the Guardian crossed the bridge, it would bring doom to her family and all of Brazil. Her mission was to protect and save her lineage, just as Gandalf's mission was to protect the Fellowship and ensure the quest to destroy the One Ring continued.

Fire Doors: The Symbol of Hope

Throughout their journey, the concept of "Fire Doors" became a powerful metaphor for Elara and her companions. Just as a fire door in a building is designed to withstand high temperatures and prevent the passage of fire and smoke, thereby containing the fire and allowing occupants to escape safely, Elara's resolve served as a spiritual fire door for her family. Her defiant stand against the curse's dark flames echoed the purpose of a fire door: to protect and preserve life, to hold back destruction, and to provide a path to safety and redemption.

Gandalf's Stand: An Inspiration

As Elara and her companions neared the heart of the Acaraí Mountains, they encountered the Guardian at a narrow bridge spanning a deep chasm. The scene mirrored Gandalf's famous stand on the Bridge of Khazad-dûm. The Guardian, a towering, demonic being of fire and shadow, bore down upon them, threatening to extinguish their hope. Elara, drawing upon Gandalf's words, stood her ground. "You shall not pass!" she declared with unwavering resolve.

The Guardian's presence was overwhelming, much like Durin's Bane, the Balrog of Morgoth. As Gandalf had done, Elara understood that if the Guardian crossed the bridge, it would bring doom to her family and all of Brazil. Her mission was to protect and save her lineage, just as Gandalf's mission was to protect the Fellowship and ensure the quest to destroy the One Ring continued.

Protection and Self-Sacrifice

Elara's allies fought valiantly to hold back the dark minions, but the true battle was between Elara and the Guardian. Elara struck the bridge with her enchanted sword in a moment of pure courage and self-sacrifice, causing it to crack and break under the Guardian's feet. The Guardian plummeted into the chasm, its fiery form consumed by the darkness below. However, as it fell, it lashed out, pulling Elara towards the abyss.

In a scene reminiscent of Gandalf's fall, Elara's bravery delayed the Guardian long enough for her allies to escape, seemingly almost at the cost of her own life. But her sacrifice was not in vain.

Fire Walls – Confronting Your Enemy

Elara's fall into the chasm seemed like the end, but she was not dead. Miraculously, she found herself on a narrow ledge, battered but alive. She saw her allies frantically searching for her from the bridge above. Summoning her remaining strength, she climbed back to rejoin them. The Guardian's defeat had bought them time, but Elara knew the curse was still not fully broken. They had more to confront.

If You Don't Do It, No One Else Will

Elara realized that breaking the generational curse required confronting the deep-seated truths of her family's past. Just as Esther in the Bible had to accept the weight of her assignment to save her people, Elara understood that she alone had the strength and determination to confront and dismantle the curse that plagued the Menendez lineage. The responsibility weighed heavily on her, but she accepted it with resolve, knowing that if she did not act, no one else would.

Esther's story resonated deeply with Elara. In the biblical narrative, Esther was placed in a position of influence for a divine purpose. She faced immense risk in revealing her identity and pleading for her people. Yet, she did so with the famous words, "If I perish, I perish" (Esther 4:16). Elara drew strength from Esther's courage and the realization that her own position and journey were no accident.

Confronting the Truths

Elara and her companions continued their journey through the Acaraí Mountains, eventually reaching a hidden cavern that housed the dark entity with which Carlos had made his pact. The cavern was filled with remnants of the past: cursed artifacts, faded portraits of ancestors, and the oppressive aura of the dark pact. Here, Elara had to confront the truths of her family's history and the choices that had led to their curse.

With her allies by her side, Elara began to destroy the cursed artifacts, each act breaking a link in the chain of the curse. As she did, memories and visions of her ancestors' sins and sufferings flooded her mind. She saw the molestations, the incest, the alcoholism, and the drug addictions. She felt the weight of generations of pain and hurt, passed down like a poisonous inheritance.

Building Fire Walls

To protect herself and her companions as they confronted each layer of the curse, Elara invoked the concept of firewalls—spiritual barriers designed to prevent the spread of the curse's influence and to compartmentalize the family's pain. Much like physical firewalls that are fire-resistant barriers designed to prevent the spread of fire between or through buildings, these spiritual firewalls were meant to contain the curse within defined sections, providing a means to tackle it piece by piece.

• Meaning: A firewall is a fire-resistant barrier that prevents fire from spreading between or through buildings. It is typically a wall that extends continuously from the foundation to the roof and is constructed to withstand fire for a specified duration, usually measured in hours.

• Purpose: Firewalls are intended to compartmentalize buildings into sections separated by these walls. In the event of a fire, the wall helps to contain the fire within one section, providing additional time for evacuation and reducing the risk of the fire spreading to other parts of the building.

Elara visualized these firewalls as she and her companions dismantled the curse's power. With each cursed artifact destroyed, she erected a spiritual firewall, sealing off the influence of that particular sin and pain from the rest of her family's legacy.

Confronting Each Layer of the Curse

1. Molestation and Incest: As Elara destroyed relics associated with these sins, she erected a firewall to contain the trauma. She envisioned the firewall stretching from the foundation of her family's history to its present, providing a barrier that prevented these particular pains from spreading further. She prayed for healing and protection for all those affected by these horrors, asking for divine intervention to stop the cycle of abuse.
2. Alcoholism and Drug Addiction: Next, she confronted the artifacts tied to substance abuse. Elara and her companions worked tirelessly to dismantle these symbols of addiction, erecting another firewall to compartmentalize this pain. She envisioned this barrier holding strong, giving her family the time and space needed to recover and break free from the chains of addiction.
3. Debauchery and Immorality: Finally, they faced the artifacts representing other immoral behaviors. Elara put up yet another firewall as each item was destroyed, isolating these influences. She called upon the strength and purity of her lineage's original virtues, reinforcing the barrier with prayers for redemption and renewal.

The Weight of the Assignment

Elara felt the weight of her assignment throughout this process, much like Esther did. The magnitude of the task and her responsibility were immense, but she knew that confronting these truths and building these firewalls were the only ways to secure a future free from the past's shadows. She felt the support of her companions, who stood by her, and the unseen strength of her ancestors, who had longed for redemption.

Elara's journey was not just about breaking a curse; it was about transforming her family's legacy from pain and suffering to resilience and hope. As she placed the final firewall, she felt a shift—a release of her heavy burden. Once oppressive and filled with darkness, the cavern now seemed lighter, as if the very air had been cleansed.

Confronting Your Past

The cavern was still and silent, but Elara could feel the weight of unfinished business pressing on her shoulders. The firewalls she erected had provided temporary protection, but she knew that more curses were rearing their heads, demanding to be confronted.

Fire Barriers – Before the Fire Doors Can Be Completely Shut

Elara believed she had broken the curse, but as the dust settled and she returned home, she realized the journey was far from over. The remnants of the curse lingered like smoldering embers, ready to ignite again if not properly contained. She needed to take further steps to ensure that the curse did not reemerge, which required the establishment of fire barriers.

Fire Barriers: Setting Up Guardrails

Elara had to put guardrails in place before the fire doors could be completely shut. These guardrails, known as fire barriers, were crucial to prevent the spread of any residual flames of the curse. Fire barriers are designed to classify areas, limiting fire spread and providing a structured defense against potential flare-ups.

• Meaning: A fire barrier is a fire-resistant structure designed to prevent fire spread within a building. Unlike a fire door, an active mechanism that can be opened and closed, a fire barrier is a passive protection measure that helps contain fires in a specific area.

• Purpose: Fire barriers provide a secondary line of defense, ensuring that even if a fire door fails or is breached, the fire cannot spread uncontrollably. This containment allows for safer evacuation and minimizes damage.

Shutting the Fire Door: An Intentional Action

Elara understood that shutting the fire door was intentional and required discipline and vigilance. If a fire breaks out and the fire door opens, her actions will determine whether the fire spreads. This metaphor extended to the spiritual and emotional fires in her life. She had to take proactive steps to maintain the barriers she had erected.

1. Emptying the Bottle: Shutting the fire door meant eliminating sources of temptation and addiction. For Elara, this involved removing alcohol from her home and seeking support for those struggling with addiction within her family. Proverbs 20:1 (ESV) states, "Wine is a mocker, strong drink a brawler, and whoever is led astray by it is not wise." She took this to heart, understanding her mission's need for sobriety and clarity.
2. Refusing to Gossip: Gossip and slander had perpetuated the curse by sowing discord and mistrust. Elara committed to shutting the fire door by refusing to engage in or tolerate gossip. Ephesians 4:29 (ESV) advises, "Let no corrupting talk come out of your mouths, but only such as is good for building up, as fits the occasion, that it may give grace to those who hear." Following this principle, she aimed to foster a culture of honesty and respect.
3. Going to Therapy: Shutting the fire door involved seeking professional help to address deep-seated issues. Elara encouraged her family members to attend therapy and counseling sessions to work through their traumas. Proverbs 11:14 (ESV) highlights the value of seeking guidance: "Where there is no guidance, a people falls, but in an abundance of counselors there is safety." Therapy became a fire barrier, providing the tools needed to cope with and overcome their past.

4. Recognizing Abnormal Practices: Elara recognized that some behaviors her family celebrated as normal were, in fact, unhealthy and destructive. Shutting the fire door meant being honest about these practices and taking steps to change them. Romans 12:2 (ESV) advises, "Do not be conformed to this world, but be transformed by the renewal of your mind, that by testing you may discern what is the will of God, what is good and acceptable and perfect." This scripture guided Elara in transforming her family's mindset and practices.

The Practical Steps

To put fire barriers in place, Elara initiated several practical steps:

- Family Meetings: Regular family meetings were established to openly discuss issues, share progress, and support one another. These meetings acted as checkpoints to ensure everyone was committed to healing.
- Accountability Partners: Each family member was paired with an accountability partner. These partnerships provided mutual support and encouragement, helping them stay on track with their commitments.
- Education and Awareness: Elara organized workshops and sessions on addiction, mental health, and healthy relationships. By increasing awareness and understanding, she hoped to equip her family with the knowledge they needed to maintain their fire barriers.

Confronting Hidden Flames

Despite establishing fire barriers, Elara knew hidden flames could still lurk in the shadows, waiting to reignite the curse. She realized true peace was made through conflict—confronting and resolving underlying issues rather than avoiding them.

Breaking the Bridge – You Shall Not Pass

The cavern was still and silent, but Elara could feel the weight of unfinished business pressing on her shoulders. The firewalls she erected had provided temporary protection, but she knew that more curses were rearing their heads, demanding to be confronted.

You Can't Keep Running Away

Elara knew that to truly break the generational curse, she had to confront her past and the demons that had chased her family for generations. "You can't keep running away," she told herself. "You have to confront your past and what's chasing you." This journey was about destroying physical artifacts and confronting the deep-rooted issues and patterns that had allowed the curse to flourish.

Peace Is Made by Conflict: Elara understood that peace was not simply the absence of conflict but the result of facing and overcoming it. Each confrontation with her family's dark past was a battle, but it was necessary to make peace with their history and pave the way for a brighter future.

Breaking the Bridge

The Guardian's fall into the abyss had symbolized a temporary victory, but Elara knew she had to break the bridge of connection to the curse entirely. "You shall not pass," she repeated, echoing Gandalf's words, understanding that breaking generational curses required recognizing patterns and behaviors welcomed through indifference and apathy.

- Recognize Patterns and Behaviors: Elara scrutinized her family's history and life, identifying the destructive patterns perpetuating the curse. She saw how systems and ideologies, whether familiar or unfamiliar, had infiltrated their lives.

- Action Beyond Prayers: Breaking a generational curse was more than just praying; it required decisive action. Elara and her allies set out to change behaviors, confront painful truths, and rebuild their lives on new, healthier foundations.

Elara realized that breaking these connections required a combination of faith and action. She called upon her companions to help dismantle the bridge connecting her family to their cursed past. Together, they worked tirelessly, breaking down the final remnants of the dark pact.

Confronting More Curses

With each layer of the curse dismantled, more sinister truths surfaced. Elara faced the deeper, more insidious curses that had taken root in her family's psyche. The process was painful, involving tears, confessions, and moments of intense emotional release. She confronted the anger, bitterness, and resentment that had festered for generations.

Systems and Ideologies: Elara realized that some curses were perpetuated by deeply ingrained ideologies and systemic issues within her family. She worked to change these mindsets, fostering a culture of openness, accountability, and love.

The Final Confrontation

As Elara and her companions continued their work, they reached the core of the curse. Here, the dark entity awaited them, embodying all the pain and suffering the Menendez family had endured. This final confrontation was the most daunting, but Elara stood firm.

• Faith and Resolve: Elara's faith had carried her this far, and now it fueled her resolve to face the entity head-on. She called upon the strength of her ancestors who had longed for redemption and upon the firewalls she had built to protect her family.

- Destroying the Core: Elara and her allies confronted the dark entity in a climactic battle. The battle was fierce, with the entity summoning all the darkness of the Menendez family's past to fight against them. But Elara, fortified by her faith and the support of her companions, struck the final blow.

The dark entity was defeated with a brilliant flash of light, and the cavern filled with peace and renewal. The curse was finally broken.

Remember Who You Are Fighting For

Elara stood amidst the remnants of the dark cavern, her body and soul weary from the battle she had just endured. She looked around at her family, who had fought bravely alongside her, and realized that their journey was not just about breaking a curse but about ensuring a better future for future generations. This fight was not just for herself but for all who came before and would come after.

As Elara reflected on her and her family's struggles, she recalled Gandalf's resolve during the battle against the Balrog. Gandalf knew that his fight was not just about him. He understood the significance of his mission and who he was fighting for. The members of the Fellowship, the people of Middle-earth, and the generations that would come after them all depended on his bravery.

Elara saw the faces of her ancestors, those who had suffered under the curse, and the younger generations who looked to her for guidance and protection. She knew that the fight to shut the fire door, erect firewalls, and put up fire barriers was not just about her own peace but for the peace and prosperity of her descendants.

A Level of Selflessness

Breaking generational curses required a level of selflessness and foresight. Elara recognized that the effects of her efforts might not be fully realized in her lifetime. Just as Gandalf had fought for the future of Middle-earth, Elara fought for her family's future.

Legacy of Peace: She imagined her grandchildren growing up in a world where peace was the norm, where the hostility, conflict, and crisis she had known were distant memories. The generations before them would have fought the battles that allowed them to rest upon a foundation of stability and harmony.

A sense of duty guided Elara's actions to those who would inherit the world she was striving to create. Her efforts to shut the fire door, erect firewalls, and establish fire barriers were acts of love and sacrifice for the future.

The Final Steps

To ensure the curse was completely eradicated, Elara and her family took the following final steps:

1. Establishing Rituals of Remembrance: They created rituals to honor their journey and remember their ancestors' struggles and triumphs. These rituals served as a reminder of the importance of vigilance and the ongoing need to protect their legacy.
2. Creating a Legacy of Healing: Elara and her family are committed to ongoing healing practices, such as therapy, open communication, and mutual support. They understood that healing was a continuous process and that maintaining their fire barriers required sustained effort.
3. Educating Future Generations: Elara documented their journey, the curse, and the steps they had taken to break it. This documentation was intended to educate future generations about their history and equip them with the

knowledge and tools to maintain the peace and stability they had fought hard to achieve.

4. Building Strong Communities: Elara recognized that breaking the curse within her family was just the beginning. She and her family worked to build strong, supportive communities around them. They reached out to others struggling with similar issues, offering their experiences and support to help others break their own cycles of pain and suffering.

Embracing the Future

As the days turned into months and the months into years, Elara witnessed the transformation of her family. The once pervasive sense of doom and despair was replaced with hope and joy. The curse, which had seemed insurmountable, had been broken through their combined efforts, faith, and determination.

Elara's descendants grew up in an environment of love and support, unaware of the battles that had been fought to secure their peace. They thrived, free from the shadows of the past, able to build their own futures on the strong foundations laid by Elara and her family.

Generational Impact: Just as Gandalf's actions had ensured the safety and future of Middle-earth, Elara's fight had secured a better world for her descendants. The peace and normalcy they enjoyed were the fruits of her labor and sacrifice.

Conclusion

Elara's journey to confront and break her family's deep-seated generational curses is a testament to the power of faith, action, and selflessness. Her determination to erect spiritual fire doors, walls, and barriers ensured a future of healing and wholeness for the Menendez family. Her journey echoes the stories of great biblical figures who faced immense challenges and responsibilities yet rose to the occasion with courage and faith.

By breaking the chains of the past and erecting fire barriers to compartmentalize and contain the generational pain, Elara ensured that the Menendez family could finally move towards a future of healing and wholeness. Her legacy would be hope, resilience, and unwavering determination, proving that even the darkest curses can be overcome with light, love, and faith.

In remembering who she was fighting for and why she was fighting, Elara found the strength to continue her mission. Her story reminds us that the battles we fight today are not just for our own peace but for the peace of future generations. Our efforts to shut the fire door, erect firewalls, and put up fire barriers may not always be seen or appreciated in our lifetime, but they create a legacy of stability and hope for those who follow. Elara's fight was a testament to the enduring power of love, faith, and selflessness.

Chapter 11:
Exit Doors

Exit Doors: Subtitled Mass Exodus, Red Pill, or Blue Pill

Introduction to Exit Doors

In both literal and metaphorical contexts, exit doors serve as crucial passageways facilitating departure from a space or situation. Physically, exit doors are designed to provide a safe and efficient route out of a building during emergencies, such as fires or other crises. These doors are strategically placed to be easily accessible and operable, ensuring occupants can vacate the premises swiftly and safely. They must adhere to strict safety codes, including being well-lit, unobstructed, and opening in the direction of the evacuation flow to prevent bottlenecks and ensure smooth egress.

In a broader sense, exit doors symbolize points of departure or transition, marking the threshold between staying within a known, perhaps comfortable environment and stepping into something new, uncertain, or transformative. This concept of an exit door is a powerful metaphor for various life decisions, where one must choose between the security of the familiar and the potential growth of the unknown.

The Matrix: Red Pill or Blue Pill

The choice between the red pill and the blue pill, as presented in the iconic scene from The Matrix, serves as a profound metaphor for such decisive moments. Morpheus offers Neo two pills: the blue pill would allow him to remain in the fabricated reality of the Matrix, living in ignorance and comfort; the red pill would lead him to the truth, to see the world as it truly is, however harsh it might be.

Blue Pill:

It represents comfort, ignorance, and the continuation of life as one knows it without the burden of uncomfortable truths.

Choosing the blue pill means staying within the confines of the familiar, where predictability and perceived safety offer a seductive reprieve from the challenges of reality.

Red Pill:

Symbolizes the pursuit of truth, no matter how challenging or disruptive that truth might be.

Taking the red pill is about embracing change, confronting previously unknown or acknowledged realities, and choosing a path of potential personal growth and enlightenment.

Application to Mass Exodus from Churches

In the context of a mass exodus from churches, these metaphorical exit doors represent a critical juncture for many believers. Individuals face a decision: stay within the church (akin to taking the blue pill) and maintain the comfort of traditional beliefs and practices, or step through the exit door (akin to taking the red pill) to explore faith and spirituality on more personal, perhaps unconventional terms.

The reasons for choosing the exit door in this scenario vary widely but often include disillusionment with institutional practices, a desire for a more authentic spiritual experience, or a response to perceived hypocrisies within church leadership. For many, walking through this exit door is not just about leaving a place of worship but about seeking a deeper, more genuine connection with the divine and a faith practice that resonates more truly with their personal beliefs and experiences.

Introduction to Justin's Journey

As we delve deeper into the themes of exit doors and the choices they represent, we introduce Justin from Austin, Texas. Justin's story is emblematic of the struggles faced by many in contemporary faith communities. Discontent with his current spiritual experiences and disillusioned by what he perceives in his local church as well as those around him, Justin stands at a pivotal crossroads. His journey offers a vivid illustration of the decision between the metaphorical red and blue pills, encapsulating the essence of the mass exodus phenomenon within modern churches.

Justin's Background and Discontent

Justin, a lifelong member of his community church in Austin, has grown increasingly unsettled. His church, once a source of inspiration and community, now seems to him stagnant and out of touch with the pressing social and spiritual issues of the day. While not necessarily wrong, Justin feels that the church's teachings fail to resonate deeply with his personal experiences and the realities of the world outside the church walls.

He observes similar patterns in neighboring churches—a focus on tradition over transformation, doctrine over genuine dialogue, and a seeming disconnect from the social justice issues that plague our society. This has led Justin to question his place within his local church and the role of organized religion in his life.

The Decision: Red Pill or Blue Pill

Faced with the existential dilemma of staying or leaving, Justin reflects on the implications of each choice:

Choosing the Blue Pill (Staying): For Justin, staying in the church could mean embracing the familiarity and community he has known all his life. It represents a choice to find contentment within the established structures, hoping to foster change from within. However, this choice also means potentially suppressing his growing doubts and discontent, which could lead to a sense of resignation rather than fulfillment.

Choosing the Red Pill (Leaving): Leaving the church represents Justin's significant leap into the unknown. While filled with uncertainty, this decision holds the promise of discovering a faith expression that resonates more deeply with his personal convictions and aspirations. However, Justin is cautious; he doesn't want to decide based solely on his current feelings of dissatisfaction. He recognizes the importance of ensuring that his new path still aligns with Christ's teachings and a biblical worldview. His desire isn't simply to find a community that matches his preferences but to pursue an authentically lived faith that genuinely reflects the values and principles taught in the Scriptures. Despite his frustrations with the apparent stagnation in his current church setting, Justin's goal isn't just to leave for the sake of leaving—he seeks a transformative, active expression of faith that challenges and changes the believer, embodying the authentic change he feels is lacking within the body of Christ.

Justin's Reflection and Consideration

As Justin grapples with his decision, he undertakes a thoughtful process of reflection and self-examination. He spends significant time engaging with the Scriptures, seeking to understand how Christ's teachings might guide his choices in this pivotal moment. His explorations extend beyond personal study; he seeks counsel from trusted spiritual leaders and engages in deep, meaningful conversations with peers who share his concerns as well as those who advocate for staying within the traditional church structure.

Justin is driven by a desire for a faith community that not only shares but actively embodies his deep-seated values on justice, community, and spiritual integrity. His pursuit is focused on finding a community that vigorously upholds the values Christ espoused about the Kingdom of God—values like compassion, mercy, justice, and unconditional love. Justin seeks a congregation that doesn't just discuss these principles theoretically but lives them out dynamically, impacting the world with Christ-like actions and attitudes.

Moving Forward

Justin's journey is emblematic of a broader movement among many believers seeking reform and authenticity in their faith expressions. His decision, whether to stay or leave, will hinge on finding a path that marries his convictions with the core principles of Christianity. He knows this decision could lead to significant personal sacrifices, including the loss of community and familiar rituals that have shaped his spiritual life. However, he is prepared to embrace these losses if they mean advancing towards a more authentic practice of his faith.

As he moves forward, Justin remains open to the possibility that his search might eventually lead him back to a transformed role within his original community or toward new horizons that offer a vibrant, active engagement with faith and life. Whatever the outcome, his journey underscores the dynamic and evolving nature of faith in contemporary society, reflecting a heartfelt quest for a deeper, more genuine connection with the teachings of Christ and the community of believers.

Standing at the Door of Uncertainty

Justin stands at a literal and metaphorical threshold, the door of uncertainty swinging silently before him. It's a heavy and significant door, much like the door referenced in Revelation 3:20, where Christ stands and knocks, seeking entry. As he ponders this scripture, Justin deeply feels the weight of its implications. Here, Christ doesn't force the door open but instead waits for it to be opened from within—a profound metaphor for Justin's own situation.

Justin's Pivotal Moment

This pivotal moment feels like a direct parallel to his spiritual journey. Christ's patient, persistent invitation resonates with Justin's current state of contemplation about his place within the faith community. He knows that opening this door could lead to new beginnings, previously untraveled paths, and unknown experiences. Yet, there's comfort in familiarity, in the known quantities of his current spiritual life, even with its frustrations and limitations.

Reflection on Revelation 3:20

As Justin reflects on Revelation 3:20, he sees it not just as an invitation from Christ to open a door but as a divine prompt to make a transformative decision. It's not merely about letting Christ into his heart; it's also about stepping out in faith, about potentially walking through an exit door to seek a deeper, more resonant expression of his faith. This scripture becomes a mirror reflecting his inner conflict between the comfort of the known and the growth that lies in the unknown.

Decision Time

With the scripture echoing in his mind, Justin understands that his decision to stay or leave is not just about discomfort with the current state of his church. It's about a deeper spiritual calling to pursue a life that fully embodies the teachings of Christ as he understands them—teachings that emphasize love, justice, mercy, and active engagement with the world.

The door of uncertainty, therefore, isn't just an exit from his current church; it's potentially an entrance into a new way of living out his faith. This door symbolizes a passage from one way of being to another, promising growth but challenging him with its newness and demands.

Embracing the Uncertainty

As he stands before this door, Justin realizes that whatever decision he makes, the act of choosing is itself a step of faith. He is reminded that faith is not static but dynamic, involving constant movement as he depends on God. Whether he decides to step through the door or to stay and seek transformation from within, he knows he is answering a call to deeper engagement with his faith.

In this moment of quiet reflection, Justin feels a quiet resolve forming. As he prepares to make his choice, Justin feels a sense of peace mingled with anticipation—a recognition that, in stepping through the door, he is also stepping closer to the heart of his faith.

Justin's Research on the Mass Exodus

As Justin stands at the crossroads of his faith journey, he broadens his perspective before making any definitive moves. Curious to understand whether his feelings are isolated or part of a larger trend, he surveys faith communities beyond his local area. His investigation reveals that many others are also leaving their churches, driven by a range of issues that resonate deeply with his own experiences.

Reaching Out to Quentin in Alabama

To gain more insights, Justin reaches out to his friend Quentin, who lives on the other side of the Bible Belt in Alabama. Quentin has been closely observing similar trends in his region and provides Justin with a comprehensive breakdown of the factors contributing to the mass exodus from churches:

1. Disillusionment with Church Leadership: Many feel that leaders fail to live up to the standards they preach, leading to a loss of trust.

2. Perceived Hypocrisy: There is a noticeable gap between the church's teachings and its members' actions, especially the leaders.

3. Church Response to Social Issues: Many are disappointed by the church's stance or lack of action on critical social issues such as immigration, racial injustices, LGBTQ+ rights, and gender equality.

4. Overemphasis on Doctrine Over Relationships: The focus often seems to be more on strict adherence to doctrine than on fostering relationships and community.

5. Failure to Address Doubts and Questions: Churches often do not provide space for members to express doubts or seek answers to difficult questions, leaving many feeling unsupported in their faith journey.

6. Polarization and Political Tension: The increasing entanglement of churches with political agendas has created divisions within congregations.

7. Spiritual Abuse: Instances of leaders manipulating or coercing members for personal gain or to maintain control.

8. Lack of Relevance: A feeling that the church is not engaging with the modern world or addressing the issues that affect everyday lives.

9. Burnout Among Church Workers and Volunteers: The high demands placed on these individuals often lead to burnout, further weakening the church's ability to serve its community effectively.

10. Church Hurt: Accumulated negative experiences within the church result in deep emotional and spiritual wounds, often without adequate support or acknowledgment from the church community.

Processing the Findings

Armed with this information, Justin feels both validated and overwhelmed. The issues Quentin highlights mirror many of his own frustrations and deepen his understanding of the complex dynamics at play. This knowledge pushes him to consider his next steps not just as personal decisions but as part of a broader movement of believers seeking authenticity and reform in their spiritual lives.

Next Steps

As Justin reflects on these conversations and data, he realizes that his next actions might involve more than just finding a new church. They might require him to engage in or even initiate discussions and actions that address these systemic issues, potentially leading to real change. His journey, therefore, might take him beyond the search for a new spiritual home to becoming an advocate for transformation within the wider faith community.

With a clearer picture of the landscape and a renewed sense of purpose, Justin feels more equipped to make a decision that aligns with his deepest convictions and his commitment to living out a faith that actively engages with the world's challenges. His conversation with Quentin has not only provided clarity but has also ignited a passion for contributing to a future where the church can better reflect the values of the Kingdom of God.

The Red Pill and Blue Pill: Awakening versus Comfort

As Justin contemplates his next steps, the metaphor of the red pill and the blue pill from The Matrix serves as a compelling framework for his decision-making process. This allegory helps him visualize his options as different paths within religious practice and fundamental choices about how he engages with his faith.

The Red Pill: Awakening to a New Reality

Choosing the red pill symbolizes Justin's potential decision to leave his current church in pursuit of a faith community that more authentically aligns with the proactive and compassionate values he holds dear. This choice is about awakening to a new reality—a reality where faith is not just about adherence to tradition but is actively engaged in addressing societal issues and embodying the teachings of Jesus in practical, impactful ways. Opting for the red pill means stepping into uncertainty and leaving the comfort of the known, yet it promises a more fulfilling engagement with his faith and the world around him.

The Blue Pill: Embracing Comfort and Tradition

Conversely, taking the blue pill would mean staying within his current church or a similar environment, where the comfort of tradition and the familiar prevail. This path would require Justin to work towards change from within, confronting and hopefully transforming entrenched structures and attitudes over time. It's a safer, more predictable path but one that may require significant patience and resilience to bring about real change.

Correlation with Exiting the Church

The choice between the red pill (awakening to a new kind of faith practice) and the blue pill (remaining within the comfort of traditional structures) mirrors the decisions facing many in the broader church community. Those who feel a deep disconnect with the traditional church model often choose the red pill, leaving to explore or create new forms of faith communities that strive to live out the gospel in ways that resonate more deeply with contemporary societal challenges. Those who choose the blue pill often see value in the existing structures and feel called to nurture growth and reform from the inside.

Engaging with the Community

To refine his decision, Justin engages in discussions with a variety of individuals, including those who have left the church, those who remain, and leaders within various congregations. These conversations reveal diverse perspectives on the church's role in society and the potential for internal reform versus the need for new expressions of faith.

Reflection and Decision

Following these dialogues, Justin enters a period of introspection. He evaluates his resources, his spiritual desires, and the potential impact of his choices. In seeking guidance through prayer and reflection, Justin focuses on finding a path that aligns with his belief in a faith that is actively lived and transformative.

Ultimately, the decision between the red and blue pills transcends personal preference; it reflects Justin's commitment to a faith that not only preaches the values of the Kingdom of God but actively practices them. He acknowledges that whether he pioneers new forms of the church or revitalizes it from within, his journey will be guided by a desire to embody Christ's teachings authentically.

With resolve and clarity, Justin is ready to make his choice, understanding that it is not merely about personal fulfillment but about contributing effectively to the broader narrative of faith in today's world.

Biblical Choices and Exit Doors

As Justin contemplates his next steps, he reconnects with Quentin to explore deeper biblical insights that mirror their own dilemmas. They decide to examine the stories of biblical figures who faced pivotal decisions akin to the red pill and blue pill choices. This exploration aims to provide a spiritual framework that could guide their understanding of the mass exodus from churches they are witnessing.

Abraham's Journey: Genesis12:1-4, Justin starts the conversation by reflecting on Abraham's decision to leave Ur, as recounted in Genesis. He sees Abraham's choice to leave everything familiar behind as the quintessential red pill decision — stepping into the unknown on faith alone. Justin notes Abraham didn't just leave a place; he left what he knew was a promise. It's about trusting in God's promises more than our comfort zones.

Moses's Choice: Exodus 3:1-12, Quentin adds to the discussion by bringing up Moses. He describes how Moses, once an Egyptian prince, chose to embrace his true identity and mission despite the initial comfort and safety of the palace. Moses's decision to return to Egypt after meeting God at the burning bush," Quentin argues, "was about embracing a difficult truth over personal comfort, much like facing the realities that challenge our faith communities today."

Ruth's Loyalty: Ruth 1:16-17, The conversation then turns to Ruth, who Quentin describes as making a red pill choice in the midst of personal tragedy. According to Quentin, Ruth's decision to stay with Naomi instead of returning to Moab represents a deep faith commitment, choosing uncertainty and a new faith community over the easier path of returning to her old life.

The Rich Young Ruler's Hesitation: Mark 10:17-22

Justin reflects on the story of the rich young ruler, noting it as a blue pill choice where the ruler opts for the comfort of his wealth over the challenging path of discipleship Jesus offers. "It's a stark reminder," Justin deliberates, "of how our comforts and possessions can hold us back from fully embracing the call to follow Christ.

In the Israelites' Yearning for Egypt: Numbers 14:1-4, Quentin points out that the Israelites in the wilderness frequently lamented their freedom due to the uncertainties they faced, expressing a desire to return to slavery in Egypt where their basic needs were met. "Their preference to return to known hardship over trusting in God's provision in the wilderness mirrors the blue pill choice of clinging to the familiar, even when it's detrimental," Quentin explains.

Saul's Reign: 1 Samuel 15:10-23. Lastly, Justin discusses King Saul, whose reign was marked by decisions that prioritized his own judgment over God's commands. "Saul's choices illustrate how power and status can cloud our judgment, leading us to make choices that preserve our current circumstances rather than embracing God's will for us," he concludes.

Reflection and Application

These biblical narratives help Justin and Quentin contextualize the modern-day exodus they are studying. They see parallels in how today's church members might be facing similar red or blue pill decisions: whether to leave their spiritual comfort zones to seek a more authentic faith expression or to stay and work within existing structures despite misgivings.

This deep dive into scripture fortifies Justin's resolve and clarifies the spiritual dimensions of the decisions before him. As they conclude their discussion, both Justin and Quentin feel more equipped to make informed choices about their spiritual paths, inspired by the courage and faith of those who walked similar paths millennia ago. This biblical perspective enriches their understanding of what it means to choose between the red pill of awakening to new spiritual realities and the blue pill of remaining in tradition's comfort.

Pivotal Matrix Moment

During their discussion, Justin and Quentin circle back to a pivotal statement from The Matrix that has deeply resonated with them: I can only show you the door. You're the one that has to walk through it. This line, spoken by Morpheus to Neo, encapsulates the essence of the choices they have been exploring, both biblically and within their current church contexts.

The Door as a Metaphor for Choice

As they reflect on this statement, they recognize that the door represents more than just an exit or an entrance; it symbolizes the threshold of decision that each individual must cross of their own volition. Just as Neo had to make the choice to embrace or reject the reality revealed by the red pill, each believer must decide how to respond to the truths and challenges presented in their faith journey.

Justin's Insights: Justin shares how this metaphor of the door aligns with his feelings of standing at a crossroads. He notes that Morpheus isn't just offering a choice between two realities but also emphasizing personal responsibility in that choice. No one else can walk through that door for me. It's a decision that requires personal commitment and action.

Quentin's Perspective: Quentin agrees, adding that this moment in the movie highlights the importance of agency and the courage to embrace the unknown. It's about taking ownership of our faith journey, Quentin reflects. "Whether it's deciding to leave, stay, or transform from within, the act of walking through the door is a powerful step toward personal and spiritual autonomy."

Applying the Metaphor to Their Spiritual Journeys

Justin and Quentin see parallels between Neo's journey in The Matrix and their spiritual explorations. They discuss how believers today are often presented with doors—opportunities to change, grow, or radically alter their faith approach. Each door requires a proactive decision; no one else can make that choice for them.

The Challenge of Choosing

They contemplate the courage it takes to make such choices, recognizing that walking through the door involves risks. There are no guarantees on the other side, just the promise of authenticity and the potential for a more resonant spiritual life. This is the crux of their ongoing discussions about the mass exodus from churches—believers finding doors in their paths and deciding whether to stay in familiar territory or step into new realms of faith expression.

Moving Forward with Intention

As their discussion continues, Justin and Quentin resolve to approach their decisions with intentionality and faith. They recognize that whatever choices they make—whether to advocate for change within their churches or to seek new spiritual communities—they are responsible for taking those steps themselves.

This conversation reaffirms their resolve to be active participants in their spiritual journeys, inspired by the biblical figures they discussed and guided by the profound metaphor of the door from The Matrix. They are reminded that faith is not passive; it requires active engagement and the willingness to step through doors, embrace the unknown, and live out the convictions they hold dear.

Personal Reflections on Leaving or Staying in the "Hospital"

As Justin and Quentin delve deeper into the metaphor of the church as a hospital, they begin to personalize the implications of this analogy in their own lives. They find themselves at a crossroads, each standing at the threshold, contemplating whether to leave the hospital or to stay and fully engage with the healing process it offers.

Justin's Dilemma: To Stay or Depart

As they discuss the metaphor, Justin feels the weight of his potential departure more acutely. He sees an early exit as akin to pulling out the IV and stopping the medicines prematurely. He recognizes his own unmet needs and the disillusionment that has crept into his faith experience. The church, his spiritual hospital, seems no longer capable of addressing his deepest spiritual ailments, leaving him feeling neglected and isolated. Yet, he wonders if leaving now might mean missing out on a deeper healing that could take place with more time and patience. Am I giving up too soon? Justin asks himself, pondering the risk of stepping out in search of a new path that might offer a more authentic engagement with his faith.

Quentin's Reflection: The Risk of Premature Exit

On the other hand, Quentin grapples with the fear of what leaving might mean for his spiritual life. He questions whether he's rejecting necessary care by considering an exit. Could my frustrations be addressed if I advocate for change from within? he considers, weighing the possibility of healing through transformation rather than departure. Quentin worries about the spiritual repercussions of walking away from a community that, despite its flaws, has been his home and sanctuary.

The Danger of Self-Diagnosis

Both friends confront the danger inherent in self-diagnosis. They discuss how leaving the church—rejecting the care of their spiritual leaders—might lead to spiritual isolation and the mismanagement of their faith healing process. Are we qualified to guide our own spiritual recovery without the support of a community? Justin ponders, acknowledging the risks of navigating their spiritual journeys without the structure and support of the church.

The Decision at the Door

Standing at the decision door, Justin and Quentin realize that their choices carry significant personal and spiritual consequences. This door symbolizes a physical exit and a departure from a familiar way of experiencing and practicing faith. It's a point of profound personal decision—whether to stay and seek healing within the known confines of their church or to step out into the uncertainty of a new spiritual landscape.

Weighing Heartbreak against Potential Growth

The potential heartbreak of a premature exit looms large. They reflect on the deep connections and shared histories within their church community. Leaving could sever ties that have been sources of comfort and support through life's challenges. Yet, the allure of finding a community that aligns more closely with their understanding of what a faith community should embody—compassionate, active, and transparent—motivates them to consider the red pill.

Reflections

As their discussion continues, Justin and Quentin feel a renewed sense of clarity about the gravity of their choices. They agree to take more time for prayer and reflection, seeking guidance from both within and from trusted mentors and peers. Whatever their final decisions, they resolve these choices with a deep commitment to their spiritual health and growth, ensuring they are not just reactions to pain but thoughtful responses to their callings.

Their journey through the metaphor of the church as a hospital has illuminated the challenges they face and the potential paths forward, highlighting the need for courage, patience, and an unwavering pursuit of spiritual authenticity in their decisions.

Exploring Spiritual Thresholds: Revelation 3:20 and Exit Doors"

The discussions between Justin and Quentin and their reflections on the metaphor of the church as a hospital find a profound connection in Revelation 3:20. This scripture states: "Behold, I stand at the door and knock. If anyone hears my voice and opens the door, I will come into him and eat with him, and he with me." This verse can be seen as a pivotal element that ties together their spiritual dilemmas and the choices they face at their respective "exit doors."

In the context of their metaphorical hospital, Revelation 3:20 symbolizes a constant divine presence and invitation at every exit door within their spiritual journey. Christ stands at the threshold, not pushing the door open but knocking, offering to enter into deeper fellowship with anyone who chooses to open the door. This portrays a relationship that respects personal agency and underscores the importance of personal choice in spiritual matters.

The Door as a Point of Decision

For Justin and Quentin, each exit door they contemplate—whether it leads out of the church or deeper into it—represents a point of decision where Christ's invitation must be considered. It's not just about choosing to stay or leave based on personal or communal issues; it's about discerning how Christ is calling them through these decisions:

• For Justin, considering the red pill, the door represents a potential exit from the traditional church setting, which might feel like stepping away from a known spiritual treatment plan. Yet, Revelation 3:20 reassures him that Christ is present even in this decision, knocking and ready to enter into a new type of fellowship with him outside the traditional walls.

• For Quentin, contemplating the blue pill, the door is an entrance deeper into the life of his current church. It is an invitation to open wider to Christ's healing within the existing structure and to work for transformation from within, influenced by the continual knocking of Christ and seeking to enrich his spiritual journey there.

The Impact of Opening the Door

In both cases, opening the door does not simply mean accepting Christ in a general sense; it means engaging deeply with His presence and calling in the specific context of their challenges and decisions. For both men, opening the door might mean:

• Embracing Change: Whether by transforming their church experiences or finding new communities where they can live out their faith more authentically.

• Healing and Fellowship: Recognizing that Christ's promise to dine with them symbolizes intimate communion and support, which can lead to healing—spiritual, emotional, and communal.

The Role of Revelation 3:20 in Their Decisions

Revelation 3:20, therefore, is not just a backdrop for their decision-making but a central component of it. It reminds Justin and Quentin that whatever door they choose to open or close, the decision should align with an invitation to deeper fellowship with Christ. It highlights the transformative potential inherent in choosing to engage with Christ's presence at these critical junctures. In essence, their responses to the exit doors— whether stepping through or closing them for deeper engagement inside—are responses to Christ's knock, a call to open to greater truth, healing, and spiritual vitality.

This scriptural reflection helps them realize that their spiritual journeys are not just about navigating institutional challenges but about continually responding to Christ's personal and persistent invitation for fellowship, wherever that may lead them.

Reflecting on Choices

As Justin and Quentin delve deeper into their exploration of spiritual exit doors and the decisions they face, they draw inspiration from the parable of the Prodigal Son in Luke 15. This biblical story presents two brothers, each embodying different responses to their life circumstances and their father's love, offering a rich allegory for understanding the dynamics of departure and dissatisfaction within the church.

The Two Sons and Their Choices

The Younger Brother's Departure: The younger brother makes a decisive choice to leave his father's home, taking his inheritance prematurely—a symbolic act of taking the red pill and stepping outside his father's protective covering. Believing he could manage life independently, he neglects and fails to appreciate all his father has done for him. His journey away from home leads him to the harsh realities of independence, culminating in a profound moment of destitution. This lowest point forces him to confront the consequences of his departure and the realization of what he had left behind.

The Older Brother's Internal Exit: Meanwhile, the older brother, who physically stays within the father's house, experiences a different kind of exit. He remains present in the home but becomes increasingly self-absorbed and detached from the essence of what his father offers. He does not take a physical exit but undergoes a mental and spiritual departure. Consumed by what he perceives as neglect, he feels overlooked and undervalued. His grievances show that one can be physically present yet emotionally and spiritually disconnected, adhering to routine and tradition without genuine engagement.

The Father's Role: A Beacon of Hope and Anticipation

The father in the parable, standing as a symbol of steadfast love and patient anticipation, embodies the ideal response of the church to those who wander away. Unlike traditional interpretations where the father welcomes the younger son back, in this narrative, the father remains on the horizon, his gaze fixed in hopeful anticipation, symbolizing his readiness to forgive and embrace should the son ever choose to return.

This depiction of the father highlights a profound lesson for the church: to maintain an open, welcoming stance even when departures seem definitive. His unwavering position on the horizon is a powerful reminder of the church's role to continually offer a place of return, a sanctuary of acceptance and forgiveness, regardless of how far or long a member might stray.

A Continuous Presence of Love: Embracing Both Sons

In the narrative of the father and his two sons, the continuous presence of the father's love extends equally to both the son who leaves and the son who stays. Even though the older son remains at home and fulfills his duties, he experiences his own form of internal exit, becoming emotionally and spiritually detached from the heart of the family. Despite this, the father's love for him remains unwavering, demonstrating an important dimension of divine love — it is inclusive and steadfast, regardless of external compliance or internal disconnection.

Unconditional Love for the Dutiful Son

The father's approach to the older son, who remains physically present but is internally distant, underscores a profound lesson for the church: love and acceptance must extend beyond mere physical presence or the fulfillment of duties. The father's love is not conditioned on the older son's performance or visible commitment. Instead, holistic love seeks to engage him at a deeper emotional and spiritual level.

This aspect of the father's love highlights the need for the church to nurture not just those who stray and return but also those who stay yet struggle internally. The church is called to recognize and address all members' spiritual and emotional needs, ensuring that even those who do not physically leave feel valued, understood, and deeply connected to the community.

Weaving Insights into Their Ongoing Journey

For Justin and Quentin, this expanded understanding of the father's love inspires them to consider how their churches might better support individuals like the older brother — those who are physically present but may be experiencing feelings of disillusionment or neglect. They discuss strategies for deepening engagement within the church, such as creating more open forums for expressing doubts and frustrations and implementing programs that address all congregants' emotional and spiritual well-being.

This discussion also prompts them to think about how they can contribute to a culture of inclusiveness and unconditional love as part of their church communities. They resolve to advocate for practices that recognize and honor both the visible and invisible struggles of their fellow church members, ensuring that everyone, regardless of their spiritual state, feels the continuous presence of love and acceptance.

As "Exit Doors: Mass Exodus, Red Pill or Blue Pill" draws to a close, the journeys of Justin and Quentin come to poignant resolutions, echoing the divergent paths of the brothers in the Parable of the Prodigal Son.

Justin's Decision: Embracing the Red Pill Justin, like the younger brother, chooses the red pill, deciding to step away from the familiarity and perceived safety of his current church environment. His choice is driven by a desire for authenticity and a faith practice that resonates more deeply with his personal convictions. Though his path is uncertain, Justin embraces the freedom to explore and express his faith in new and potentially fulfilling ways. His departure is a bold step into the unknown, fueled by a belief that there is more to discover beyond the traditional boundaries of his spiritual upbringing.

Quentin's Choice: Opting for the Blue Pill, Quentin, mirroring the older brother, chooses the blue pill, opting to remain within the comfort and structure of the church he knows. Despite recognizing its imperfections, Quentin believes in the potential for change from within and feels called to be a part of that transformation. His decision is marked by a commitment to deepen his engagement with the community and to work towards addressing the challenges and needs that have become apparent through his reflections and discussions with Justin.

The Father on the Horizon As both men set forth on their respective paths, the image of the father from the parable remains a powerful symbol of hope and unconditional love. Standing at the door, the father looks out onto the horizon with anticipation, hopeful for the day his son may choose to return. This enduring image of the father's steadfast gaze captures the essence of the church's role—as a beacon of grace and forgiveness, always ready to welcome back those who wander, always holding space for reconciliation and renewal.

The Sage Continues, More Will Be Revealed

Beyond The Doors: What's Next

About the Book

Beyond the Doors takes readers on a transformative spiritual journey, exploring the symbolic doors that represent various stages and challenges in our walk with God. Drawing from his personal experiences, Darick T. Fisher provides profound insights into moving beyond the initial threshold of faith, navigating the hidden traps, and confronting the moments of doubt and fear that often arise. With biblical wisdom and personal reflection, Fisher delves into the cyclical nature of spiritual growth, addressing the purifying trials that refine our faith and the barriers—both seen and unseen—that can impede our progress. He speaks to the critical importance of breaking generational curses, freeing families from the patterns of sin and suffering that can hinder their spiritual journey. Fisher also touches on the mass exodus from the church, exploring why many believers struggle with remaining faithful in times of spiritual disillusionment. He encourages readers to seek a deeper, more intimate relationship with Christ, based on Revelation 3:20, where Jesus stands at the door of our hearts, desiring communion with His children. Beyond the Doors reminds us of the importance of recognizing when God closes certain doors, and the peace that comes from trusting in His perfect timing. This book challenges and equips readers to press beyond the limitations of their past, embrace God's divine purpose, and walk confidently through the doors He opens into a deeper, more abundant life.

About the Author

Darick T Fisher is a dynamic and multifaceted individual whose life weaves a rich tapestry of diverse experiences, each thread contributing to his identity as a Pastor, Coach, Mentor, Entrepreneur, and retired Assistant Fire Chief. Married to Venus Fisher for 22 years and father of four children. His entrepreneurial spirit shines through as the proud owner of Faithful Accountable Teachable LLC, a venture that reflects his commitment to teaching and guiding others on their personal and professional journeys.

Here are a few highlights about TMM Publishing

1) We don't take out any royalties

2) You keep your intellectual property (You own your book)

3) You don't have to have a manuscript to start; you only have to have an idea. (We help you develop it)

4) You can purchase your book at wholesale price (no third party or up-charging)

5) Not only are we going to develop and publish your book, but we will help you successfully launch your book.

Are you called to write and publish? It's time to be faithful to the call.

Visit our website at www.TMMPublishing.com and book a Free 30-minute consultation. Or text " book" to (321) 471 1944

Made in the USA
Columbia, SC
07 November 2024

45953768R00137